Forms of Life

Forms of Life

The Method and Meaning of Sociology

Harry Collins

The MIT Press
Cambridge, Massachusetts
London, England

This book was set in ITC Stone Sans Std and ITC Stone Serif Std by Toppan Best-set Premedia Limited.

Library of Congress Cataloging-in-Publication Data

Names: Collins, H. M. (Harry M.), 1943– author.
Title: Forms of life : the method and meaning of sociology / Harry Collins.
Description: Cambridge, MA : The MIT Press, [2019] | Includes bibliographical
    references and index.
Identifiers: LCCN 2018026969 | ISBN 9780262536646 (pbk. : alk. paper)
Subjects: LCSH: Sociology—Methodology.
Classification: LCC HM511 .C6573 2019 | DDC 301.01—dc23 LC record available
    at https://lccn.loc.gov/2018026969

10 9 8 7 6 5 4 3 2 1

Contents

1   Introduction

Hints and Guidelines Extracted from Chapter 1

- Three activities make up the foundations of sociological method:
  - Immersing oneself in society
  - Estranging oneself from society
  - Explaining what has been discovered to those who have not been immersed
- The meaning of *science* has changed since the 1970s.
- The fractal model is needed to understand social groups.
- "Subjective" methods can be scientific and stronger than "objective" methods.
- Even physics is based on subjective social judgments.
- Life depends on the sociological meta-expertise of knowing how far social groups extend.
- What stereotyping means.
- Our understanding of life is undersocialized, not oversocialized.
- We can use numbers to persuade as well as discover.
- Science is a handy domain for studying knowledge in general.

A Simple Approach

The number of social science methods texts and handbooks is large and growing. It must be daunting to students and professionals alike to face this torrent of writings—it certainly frightens me. But the principles of social science methods are simple and, I believe, timeless, in spite of the churn of sociological fashion. The lasting heart of sociology as a unique discipline with its own identity is the idea of the social. The starting point

is Durkheim, along with the sociology of knowledge: humans are constituted by societies. From here, the methods can be worked out from first
principles. That is what the book is about, but the discrete methodological hints and guidelines that can be pulled out of the discursive argument
are listed at the head of each chapter. As the large literature on methods
indicates, there are as many minor variants of social science advice as there
are fieldwork situations; but we will look at the big picture, taking the lead
from experience, that experience being based on the idea of sociology as a
unique study of forms of life, or collectivities of human beings engaged in
social life. There is no other science that studies social life as a basic con-
stituent of the world.

The three elements of method that build on this foundation are:

1. Learn to understand a social group by becoming a member of it.
2. Accomplish estrangement from it and then reflect.
3. Communicate the outcome persuasively to those who do not
    understand.

A crucial question concerns the depth of stage 1. My own studies range
from total failure to understand anything to what we now call "contributory expertise"—learning enough to contribute to the domain being studied. In between, and the most important idea, is "interactional expertise,"
which is about becoming fluent in the language of the domain. One of my
studies, based on interactional expertise, has been going on for forty-five
years to date. But socialization to the point of near-complete interactional
expertise is beyond many researchers, while most student projects won't go
further than a few interviews. But, as we will see, this is not fatal: the crucial
thing is to know what one is trying to do, understand the compromises,
and present the results honestly. Given this, solid results can be obtained
with very few resources.

In my experience, one can work out what to do in practice using only
a couple of ideas that grow out of the basic concept of sociology. I leaned
heavily on one or two books: Peter Winch's *The Idea of a Social Science*,
and, to a lesser extent, Peter Berger's *Invitation to Sociology*. Neither of these
books is about the kind of methods found in methods textbooks; what they
do is take a broad, philosophical view of the nature of social life. By starting with principles in this way, rather than with narrow recipes meant to
fit preplanned fieldwork situations, one can work out how to proceed in

real time given the inevitable unpredictability of fieldwork. The carefully executed field study that nicely follows the initial plan is a stranger to my research life. Nevertheless, there may be something to be learned from the extensive experience of someone like me: I try to show how to approach things, if not how to plan.

Since the major driver of this book is experience, and since experience has different lessons to teach at different stages of a research career, here and there the book has an autobiographical flavor. At the start of any career, one tends to be uncertain and short of resources; at the end, one is secure and, with luck, has time and money to do what one wants. At the start of my career, the sociological community was working in the benign political atmosphere of the 1960s and '70s; now we live under the malign threat of populism and its potential aftermath, and this changes the gaze. Many of the ideas presented here have already been published, and some, notably some of the gaze-changing ones, are in the process of being published, but pretty well every word has been written from scratch. The publications of mine that have made marked contributions to the chapters are indicated in appendix 2; thirty-five are listed, which gives an indication of the many ways experience has been used in the book's arguments.

Scientific Sociology

In the 1960s in the UK, a widely used textbook written by the late Stephen Cotgrove proclaimed it was setting out the principles of "scientific sociology."[1] What Cotgrove meant by scientific sociology was something that mimicked the procedures of physical science as it was understood at the time: subjective, qualitative investigation might be good for developing hypotheses, but the science came with the testing—using questionnaires and technically sophisticated statistical analysis of the results. This view was echoed in the powerhouses of much of the then-current social science. But new kinds of studies of scientific practice, beginning in the 1970s, have shown us that the natural sciences work very differently from the scientists' self-descriptions that were once accepted at face value by social scientists. We also now know, though it should have been obvious for decades, that the statistical guarantees of validity generally offered in the case of scientific sociology—"this result has not more than 1 chance in 20 of being due to chance"—are unreliable. When one takes into account systematic errors as well as random errors, the ubiquitous 2-sigma standard frequently gives no better than, roughly, a 50 percent chance of the findings being right; this has been shown by the continual failures of replication of 2-sigma results in disciplines where replicability is valued.[2]

But the situation is far from gloomy for the social sciences, even when they are thought of as genuine sciences. Here it will be argued that if the social sciences are properly understood, and their results soundly generated, their findings can be even more reliable than those of the physical sciences, even though some of these demand a 5-sigma, or 1-in-3.5 million, confidence level. So this book is a kind of new "science of society," but with both the natural and social science looking very different from what Cotgrove had in mind.

Insofar as this book makes a contribution to the formalized "methods" literature it is meant to indicate what ought to change in the next generation of those very large and comprehensive methods texts. It is a strange thing that one of the most successful fields of social science over the last fifty years or so has been the social study of science, and yet the results have not been absorbed into the discipline as a whole. The idea of science that informs both the philosophy of social science and social science methods seems unchanged; they are still dealing with the problems I was made to study as an undergraduate. Admittedly, social science methods have moved a long way in the qualitative direction but, on the journey, the field has given up its claim to being a science. Here I argue that sociology is qualitative at its heart but, nonetheless, it should be proud to call itself a science because we now know much better what science means.

The claim about the scientific reliability of the social sciences that has just been made, and how different it is from the old model, can be illustrated by an anecdote. I have spent a good bit of my career investigating the physics of the detection of gravitational waves—the forty-five-year study mentioned earlier. I have been investigating this field since 1972 and was more or less embedded in the community that made the first detection.[3] Around the year 2000, Gary Sanders, at that time project director of the Laser Interferometer Gravitational-Wave Observatory (LIGO), and I were having lunch in the Livingston LIGO installation, about a forty-minute drive from Baton Rouge, Louisiana. He was ragging me in a good-humored way about the weakness of what he saw as my "sociological method." As he put it, this amounts to "asking a few people what they think and recording it as a finding if two or three of them agree." I replied that it was a bit more complicated and, actually, my methods were more robust than his. As an example, I said that even though I'd never used public transport in Louisiana, I was ready to bet on the basis of my sociological understanding that I could not get on a bus in Baton Rouge and buy two tickets, one for me and one to reserve the seat next to me and keep it empty.[4] I pointed out that, furthermore, the two of us were more certain about this than we would be about the validity of the discovery of the first gravitational wave. He saw the point and, remarkably, the point has now been demonstrated! As someone embedded in that whole discovery process I can tell you that in the three months after September 14, 2015, when the first signal that would survive criticism and be counted as a real gravitational wave was glimpsed, there was more nervousness about the upcoming proclamation of the discovery than about what you could do when you boarded a Baton Rouge bus. Though only the insiders, like me, knew this, the nervousness did not dissipate until a second, unannounced gravitational wave was seen on December 26.[5]

Investigating Collectivities

So how is it that a simple claim about buses in Baton Rouge, based on no local empirical evidence, can be so much more certain than the first observation of a billion-dollar international physics research program? We have to start with the foundations of sociology.

One science can be distinguished from another according to their fundamental units of investigation: physics begins with the smallest things—quarks or strings; chemistry builds up from quantum states; biochemistry starts with molecules; biology starts with cells; medicine starts with organs; psychology begins with the behavior of entire, usually human, organisms; social psychology investigates the interaction between human organisms; but sociology starts with collectivities of humans—Germans, English; cricketers, footballers; Catholics, Protestants, Muslims; scientists, artists; physicists, chemists; gravitational wave physicists, nuclear physicists; dwile flonkers; and so on. These groups overlap, and are usually subdividable and embedded within one another; but sociology starts, or ought to start, by treating each of them, at whatever level, as distinctive and irreducible ways of being in the world.[6] Under this model, sociology's claim to be a unique science comes from the way it treats humans: instead of treating humans as the elements that constitute social collectivities, it treats *humans as made out of collectivities*—as made up of things that are larger than themselves rather than smaller: for sociology the molecule is the individual, and the atoms that compose it are these big things called collectivities. This is the "ontology" that makes sociology a special science. An analogy might help. An individual speaker of a natural language exemplifies the collectivity of English speakers in much the same way as a thermometer in a beaker of liquid exhibits the temperature; the temperature belongs not to the thermometer but to the liquid. Just as a thermometer gets the temperature from the substance in which it is immersed, so a native language speaker gets natural language from the linguistic collectivity into which he or she is immersed and from which language speaking abilities are drawn. Thus, in such cases, when one examines an individual, one sees not the individual but the embodiment of the collectivity, *or set of collectivities*, from which that individual is made.[7]

The point is represented in figure 1.1, in which we imagine a set of overlapping and mutually embedded collectivities—the variously shaded shapes—and an individual who partakes in each of them.[8] You can be a German, footballing Christian who is a chemist, or you might be an English, cricketing, Muslim artist. What sociology does is investigate, at any level, how one becomes one of these things and what it means to be one. To formalize this idea, one would need to draw on esoteric domains of physics or mathematics because the diagram should not be two-dimensional but multidimensional, with complex embeddings and overlappings; but the two-dimensional simplification is more than good enough for all practical and theoretical purposes, so long as one is ready for some rough edges.

Incidentally, if you look at how we can assemble an individual person out of the lists of collectivities mentioned above—the molecule out of the atoms—you can see that it would just about be possible to be a German cricketer, except that cricket is not much played in Germany. It is the things that are done that are typical of a society that constitute the society. Being a cricketer is not constitutive of being a German whereas, to some extent, being a footballer is. Or, to repeat an example I have used frequently, *as a member of the Azande* you can divine a witch but you cannot take out a mortgage, whereas *as a British person* you can take out a mortgage but you

Figure 1.1
The individual is the sum of the collectivities in which they share.

cannot divine a witch; divining witches is constitutive of being a member of the Azande but not of being British, and taking out a mortgage is constitutive of being British but of not being an Azande.[9]

There are many starting points for the philosophical understanding of what it is to be a social collectivity.[10] I'll mention the one that happens to have informed my thinking since 1967: Wittgenstein's notion of *form of life* (see, e.g., *Philosophical Investigations*, 1953). I chanced on it in Peter Winch's book, *The Idea of a Social Science*, which was published in 1958. I already had a degree in sociology so was ready to relate what I was reading to Durkheim and the sociology of knowledge, but it was Winch who turned my head in the direction it has been pointing ever since. According to Winch, what it is to belong to a form of life is to share the concepts and engage in the actions that define that collectivity. Investigating the concepts that define the collectivity and investigating the actions that define the collectivity are just two sides of the same coin, as the actions make no sense without the concepts and the concepts make no sense without the actions; the two taken together constitute the form of life.[11]

The example that Winch used, anticipating Thomas Kuhn's notion of paradigms, which are best understood as forms of life within science, was the way the form of life of medicine changed when the germ theory of disease was invented. We now see surgeons engaging in almost ritualistic scrubbing and cleansing before they operate: all that scrubbing is part and parcel of our notion of germs—it shows what germs are—while at the same time the scrubbing arises out of the notion of germ. We couldn't have hygiene without the idea of germs, and we couldn't have the idea of germs without the scrubbing.

Incidentally, the organization of this very book is based on the same idea: I will be talking sometimes about how to do sociology and sometimes about how to think about it—the "method" and "meaning" of the subtitle. Since method and meaning are but two sides of the same coin when it comes to the form of life of sociology, I will be switching between them whenever it is explanatorily convenient.

The Fractal Model

The *fractal model* resolves potential confusion about what it is to be a form of life or collectivity and indicates another reason why figure 1.1 would be multidimensional in a mathematically perfect world. One might ask whether a form of life is something big, like *native English speakers*, or something small, like *surgeons operating under the germ theory of disease*. One might ask whether being a member of a form of life is something like *being Christian* or something like *being a person who has been trained through apprenticeship to be good at taking a blood-pressure reading*. The fractal model simply says that all of these are forms of life, and, as already intimated, these overlap and are embedded within one another in a complex way. Notice that skills and types of expertise, such as surgery or blood-pressure measurement, are treated as forms of life along with other features of culture: the acquisition of skills and expertise is treated as a process of socialization into specialist domains, and this has given rise to a useful understanding and classification of expertise known as the Periodic Table of Expertises.[12]

Why "fractal model"? Some well-known examples of fractal structures are cauliflowers, where there are florets, within florets, within florets, exhibiting the same geometry at every scale, and the coast of Norway, where there are fiords, with coastlines containing smaller fiords, which have mini-fiords within them, and so on. The mathematical idea of the fractal is drawn on here because, at every level and every scale, forms of life have the same basic properties: one comes to inhabit them through a process of socialization, and they are characterized by specialist bodies of tacit knowledge and implicit understandings that are hard or impossible to convey by formal means. But remember: we are dealing with an analogy here, not an exact mathematical model, and it won't always work perfectly because of the multiple dimensions of embedding.

In real life, as opposed to mathematical abstraction, a fractal has to come to an end somewhere. At the smallest level, the cauliflower won't exhibit ever-more miniaturized florets but finishes with a few individual cells, and the coast of Norway eventually becomes just grains of sand as you magnify further and further. The same goes for social life—if you go down low enough, it ceases to be social life and becomes a collection of a few human organisms.

Figure 1.2 is a depiction, in only two dimensions of course, of UK society and a few of its embedded collectivities. The topmost oval represents

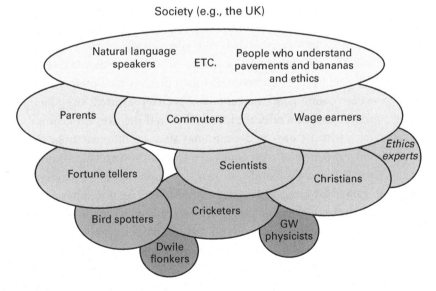

Figure 1.2
The fractal model of society.

what, in other sociological approaches, would be called the "national culture," but because of the way types of expertise and cultures are treated
as the same in this way of thinking, the top oval can be thought as representing a collection of "ubiquitous expertises"—types of expertise that
are acquired by all the citizens of a society as well as the esoteric groups
within it. Ubiquitous expertises include native-language-speaking citizens'
general understanding of how close to walk to others on the pavement
(sidewalk) depending on how crowded it is—something that will vary from
society to society. UK citizens' ubiquitous expertise includes an understanding of the proper shape of bananas in contrast with European bureaucrats'
understanding of the shape—at least, it was said to be involved when the
bureaucrats tried to impose rules for banana shapes on UK imports (possibly a mythical story, but nationalist newspapers were sure that UK citizens
were the true experts on the proper curvature of bananas). Finally, though
of course we could find an indefinite number of examples, understanding
of proper ethical behavior has to be ubiquitous if a nation is to justify its
criminal justice system—people have to know what is right and wrong if
they are to be punished for doing wrong. The idea of ubiquitous expertises has proved fruitful in the philosophical understanding of expertise,
which otherwise gets pulled toward the idea that expertises are, by definition, esoteric and hard won in adulthood, and necessarily involve excel-
lence and a superior understanding of truth; this leads to problems and
paradoxes, since our idea of what is true keeps changing and experts disagree all the time. The other ovals lower down the fractal should be largely
self-explanatory; hygienic surgery and blood-pressure measurement, since
they have been mentioned, could also have been represented. The italicized
"*Ethics experts*" indicates ethical philosophers and the like, who comprise
a collectivity with its own understandings that are different from those
of ubiquitous expertise in ethics but have an interesting relationship with
them. The bottom entry, "Dwile flonkers," refers to a group of players of a
made-up game that involves flinging a beer-soaked rag into other players'
faces (you can check it on Google), which probably does not quite comprise
a social group and so probably slips off the bottom of the fractal—like cells
in a cauliflower or sand in a Norwegian fiord. Dwile flonkers are there just
to show where the fractal comes to an end.[13]

How might we draw a stick figure on figure 1.2 to show how an individual is made up of the collectivities available in his or her society? It would

be difficult—the body would have to bend all over the place depending on which elements of the fractal it belonged to, but somehow all the citizens in a society would have all of themselves in the top level while only bits of themselves in the various lower levels, and so on. One needs not to be too pedantic in using this model—just accept that it works in a number of different ways at the same time.

To investigate these things—and this is the basic method of sociology—the sociologist uses the same method as you used, reader, when you grew up as a child and became a member of your native society: *to investigate a collectivity you become a member of that collectivity via the process of socialization.* Once you are a member, you know the concepts and the typical actions that belong to the collectivity. If you do it thoroughly you will possess what we now call "interactional expertise" (chapter 4), which is the ability to speak the language fluently of whatever domain you are investigating, and speaking the language fluently means understanding what there is to be understood about the domain. That is why sociological knowledge can be so reliable and why I had an answer for Gary Sanders.

Knowing something sociological is like getting into a swimming pool. What you know when you get into a pool is what it feels like to be wet, and that is about as fundamental a kind of knowledge as there is. Both Gary Sanders and I knew what it was like to get into the "swimming pool" of bus rides in our society, and that is why we were so certain about what was going to happen in Baton Rouge even though neither of us had ever used public transport in that town. The reason why that knowledge could be more certain than the first outcome of a billion-dollar international physics research program aimed at the detection of gravitational waves is that physicists cannot immerse themselves in the life of gravitational waves; everything they know about gravitational waves they know "from the outside," using various kinds of measurement, calculation, and inference, without ever getting into the swimming pool. The only pool they can swim in, as physicists, is *their social lives as physicists*; they have much less in the way of direct access to the physical world than sociologists have to the social world. Incidentally, the physicist and the sociologist of physics share direct experience of the social world of physicists once the sociologist has become satisfactorily socialized into it.

Interestingly and importantly, one of the things that the physicists had to establish before they could announce that they had truly seen a gravitational wave was that it was not a false signal inserted maliciously into the apparatus by hackers. This involved a long and careful reconstruction of all the ways the hack could have been achieved and what the hackers would have to have known to accomplish it. The conclusion was that it was possible but that it would have required a conspiracy by a fairly large number of expert members of the detecting team. It was agreed that such an extensive conspiracy was implausible. So the confidence in the detection depended, in the last resort, on a judgment based on the physicists' immersion in their own social life![14]

It is really odd that physics knowledge should ever have been taken to be more reliable than knowledge based on this kind of much more immediate social experience. The reason is probably that one kind of knowledge is said to be "subjective" and the other is said to be "objective," and we have come to distrust the subjective. We'll come back to that point a little later, but, since we now know that the judgments that physicists make are themselves set in the context of the social life of physics, there is no escape from this kind of subjectivity.

The accusation of "subjectivity" aside, isn't there a problem with the certainty of our knowledge about buses in Baton Rouge given the lack of *local* knowledge? Neither Gary Sanders nor I had ever ridden a Baton Rouge bus! What if Baton Rouge is different from everywhere else? It could be so and, likewise, the wetness of the next swimming pool might be different from the wetness of all the others. Suppose, for example, someone has filled the next pool with water from the Dead Sea—it is going to feel a bit different. And something similar goes for buses in Baton Rouge. But no knowledge is completely certain. We can live only because we ignore most of the logically possible uncertainties or, at least, have ways of thinking about what is a good bet and what is a bad one as far as the future is concerned. We aren't really in doubt about what the next swimming pool is going to feel like, and we also have a kind of tacit sociological "metaknowledge" about how widely to generalize when it comes to social understandings. If we didn't have that sociological metaknowledge, we would never dare go beyond our front door in case our expectations of how people in the next street were going to behave toward us turned out to be dangerously wrong. It is this that gives us the confidence to get on a bus in the first place: we believe the driver will take us to the expected destination in reasonable safety rather than, say, shutting the door and robbing us or going on a mad driving spree. I remember a Hollywood film where the taxi from Kennedy Airport had locked doors, sharpened lock-lifters, and an evil driver who took the passengers to a derelict building and shot them. Departures from reasonable expectations are rare enough to make memorable films. Mostly we have to rely on the normal being normal—we have to rely on the reliability and continuity of social life. Of course, all bets are off in times of war and revolution.

It was the kind of sociological metaknowledge that stops moment-to-moment ordinary life from being a fearsome adventure that gave Gary Sanders and me our certainty about seat reservation in Baton Rouge in particular. Nevertheless, my sociological metaknowledge also tells me not to extend that degree of certainty about bus riding to, say, Pyongyang. I would guess the nonreservability of empty bus seats would still hold in Pyongyang, but, for me, the certainty associated with the detection of the first gravitational wave is higher than my certainty about bus riding in North Korea. Some part of sociological method is going to involve thinking about the reach of one's sure sense of how collectivities work—in other words, how far does a collectivity extend? This is the problem of *uniformity*, which will be discussed in chapter 9.

Aside: Against Certain Academic Trends

At this point, it is necessary to step aside from the flow of the argument to say more about how the notion of collectivities could be misused and how this has led to trends in sociology where the notion of groups is sometimes entirely rejected. Among the "sophisticates" and "smartasses" of the early 1970s such as myself, Cotgrove's *The Science of Society* soon became a standing joke in the light of the growth of phenomenological, ethnomethodological, and other qualitative and interpretative approaches to social science. These were understood to stand in opposition not only to Cotgrove's idealized model but also to the trends in sociology rooted in the enthusiasm for science following the Second World War. The situation only became worse for these models with the development of the hugely more sophisticated understanding of the nature of science that began in the 1970s. Since that time it has become hard to proclaim the warrant of "science" for a piece of qualitative sociological work. Indeed, it would be a good bet that these days a large number of qualitative sociologists see themselves as more aligned with the humanities or more engaged in political action than pursuing a science. This leaves our subject vulnerable and with bedfellows whose embrace is generally less than welcome. The unwillingness to invoke science as a warrant is something this book is fighting; here we are saluting, once more, the unfashionable banner of a modified science of society—a more sophisticated version of the science of sociology based on a more sophisticated understanding of what science is.

The other unfashionable thing I'm doing here is proclaiming that *the very basis of sociology* is the notion of collectivity. One of the starting points of the rejection of this view is a well-known paper titled "The Oversocialized Conception of Man in Modern Sociology," published in 1961 by Dennis Wrong. Wrong complained about the oversimplification of sociology's solution to the "Hobbesian problem of order": how is it that we members of societies cooperate instead of fighting, all against all, impelled by our "animal nature"? The sociology of the time posits people as norm-internalizing and norm-following, whereas Wrong, invoking Freud, argued that the problem of why we share norms will remain unsolved until we recognize the personal and individual character of humankind.

Wrong's argument stands in stark contrast to the sociology of knowledge–based approach taken here.[15] The sociology of knowledge asks where humans' knowledge and day-to-day expectations come from and gives the only answer that can be given—it comes from the society in which we grow up or any society in which we become deeply immersed. From this point of view, both Wrong's question and his complaint seem very odd. Take natural language as the example of cooperation, and ask, "How is it that (nearly) all English persons are willing to speak only English when there are so many other languages in the world available to them?" The answer is clearly not "because they are willing norm-followers," but Wrong's complaint about individual ego isn't right either. Both sides of the debate miss the point that the only language available to nearly all native English speakers is English because that is how native English speakers are brought up. As the Tower of Babel story intimates, it takes a miracle to destroy the uniformity of natural language among those who share a society.[16] This is not, then, a matter of explaining a certain choice of action given Hobbesian concerns or Freudian propensities, because there is no choice—English is pretty well the only language available in England except for those who make a special effort to escape the determinism.

That is the sense in which individuals are the sum of the collectivities that make them up. Seen from the point of view of the sociology of knowledge, collectivities are not constraining but enabling—without them we would have no culture, no language, and no abilities beyond those of the animals: we would have no deep understanding of the world and no means to store aspects of our knowledge or to pass them on.[17]

A second source of suspicion of the primacy of collectivities comes from liberation movements that fear the undesirable political uses to which the notion of deterministic social groups can lend itself. They equate the notion that we are what we belong to with stereotyping. Stereotyping, broadly construed, is, however, the very substance of sociology; sociology generalizes about how people from "this group" versus "that group" think and act. Sometimes, however, in the course of investigating collectivities, we may find out that certain groups are more diffuse than we thought and that groups have permeable boundaries with other groups; but this does not affect the underlying logic of the science of sociology. What it does affect is the care with which the ontology should be applied in real-life situations, especially where there are political and personal implications for grouping people. Sociology is about groups and the way they work, it is not about individuals; it is when the two are confused that the damaging kind of stereotyping results. Sociology does *not* encourage anyone to understand *any particular individual's* actions as *fully explained and determined* by the groups that person comes from, but it does give them their starting point and it does explain quite a lot. In the final chapter, we'll return to the damage and political tensions that arise out of treating individuals as though they are solely members of groups and the incorrect conclusions that can be drawn from this.

Before getting back to the main theme, I'll offer another advertisement for the notion of the social collectivity and its potential. If we take the notion of the collectivity seriously, then we will conclude that entities that are primarily social will have a certain quality that is responsible for their ontology—the thing they are. Thus, philosophers and psychologists think that humans are special because they are conscious—they have a special quality called "consciousness." I presume that is true, but I also presume it is shared with at least the higher animals. The other, analogous, thing that humans have is "socialness," which is, again, a certain quality. This is not possessed by bees and ants, even though they are often referred to as social creatures, because the nature of their societies is very different—what ants and bees have is "information exchange." Socialness might be shared by some animals, for example, by apes, dolphins, and birds. One might even argue that dogs have a little socialness. But it can't be much, because given domestic dogs' continuous exposure to human social life—which is as deep and extended as that of humans—they would by now be able to speak, or at least share our norms when it comes to excretion, dress, and sex.

Animals' socialness is vestigial at best because you cannot have much socialness without rich language. Language holds human social groups together and it gives them the extraordinary qualities they have—notably mutual understanding and enough context sensitivity to know how to break rules in ways that others will understand as legitimate and innovative. Understanding this, one is in a position to say something about the peculiar nature of human social groups and what they can do that other kinds of creatures cannot do—for example, engage in complex division of labor and cooperation across large social distances. One can say, then, what entities such as intelligent computers, that are to imitate humans, will have to be able to do if they are to succeed. Thus, I am not sure if computers will have to be conscious to reproduce the subtle features of human intelligence—though I doubt it—but I am sure they will have to have socialness if they are to manage it, because so much of understanding and intelligence depends on our socialness. Socialness will be discussed again in chapter 6 and we'll come back to intelligent computers in the same place.[18]

This is a book about methods, but I include this philosophical aside because I want to show how much we'll have to give up if sociology's unique subject matter—the collectivity and the nature of the social—is surrendered. These paragraphs show just why it is important to embrace a methodology that explores the social.[19]

Estrangement and Reflection

Returning to our main theme, sociological method, as discussed here, is based on immersion in social groups. This allows socialization to take place, with the investigator aiming to become a member of the group and thus acquiring the typical understandings associated with the form of life; this is "getting into the swimming pool." But even if I know what it feels like to get into a swimming pool, do I know it in a self-conscious way? Have I ever reflected on it, or tried to describe it? The answer, in my case, if we are treating swimming pools literally, is no, at least, not until I typed these words about swimming pools in March 2017. The same applies to immersion in other previously unanalyzed collectivities. Knowing how to think and act in a society and being aware of what you know are two different things: most of what we know as we become members of a society we don't know that we know. For example, by the time you were three years old, you could form pretty good sentences in your native language but you didn't know you were putting the verb in the middle of the sentence (or wherever your native language puts it). Just think how long it took you to come to be able to articulate the rules you were applying when you spoke your native language; in fact, unless you were taught what the rules were at school, you probably still don't know, in an explicable way, how you form good sentences. What you have is mostly *tacit knowledge*. So another part of sociological method—very much parasitical on the first part—is estrangement and reflection: you have to learn to stand far enough back from what you know and then reflect on it with enough skill to come to know what you know in a self-conscious way. We'll look at this in more detail in chapter 7.

One interesting consequence of what has just been said is that, in nearly every case, you cannot find out about the nature of a collectivity simply by asking its members: *most of its members* don't know what they know or understand what they do or why they do it. There is a famous quote attributed to Richard Feynman along the lines of "Philosophy of science is as useful to scientists as ornithology is to birds," but the corollary is that just as one would not ask birds to explain ornithology, one should not ask scientists to explain science. To do science, one does not need to reflect on it, just as Feynman said; but *to understand* it analytically, one does need to reflect on it. The revolution in science studies that took place around the 1970s was the uncovering of what scientists actually did, and contrasting that with what they, and most other people—including the other academics of the time—thought and said they did.

Nevertheless, what people think they are doing is not unimportant. It reveals group members' aspirations—what they are trying to do. What people are aiming for in their lives is part of their form of life even if it does not fully describe it. The myths that pertain to a form of life tell you quite a lot about that form of life. Thus, if one asks most scientists how they know what is true and what is not, they are likely to answer something like "True findings can be replicated whereas false findings cannot, so we work out what is true by repeating our experiments and observations." Now that is a correct description of what scientists *think they are doing*, and it guides their actions in crucial ways; but, in seriously disputed areas, it is not an accurate explanation of how scientists actually reach their conclusions. Scientists cannot use replication in a straightforward way to settle their deep controversies, because in a controversial area it is impossible to be sure that an experiment has been competently performed—a problem called *the experimenter's regress*. Nevertheless, it is very important to know what scientists are *trying to do*—for example, replicate—in order to understand aspects of their society; we find scientific society continually informed by the need to replicate to be sure of things. In investigating collectivities it is very important to tease apart what we might call the "myth" from the reality, bearing in mind that the myth is also an important part of the reality. It is true that the society of scientists values replication and strives to bring it about; what is not true is that replication can always settle things in a formulaic way, even though scientists proceed as though it can.

Sorting all this out is a matter of observational and reflective expertise, but there are some tricks one can try to draw out the substance of the way people act in society. These include a couple that will be unfamiliar to sociologists who are not deeply immersed in the science studies literature, but they could nevertheless be found useful; they will be discussed in chapter 7. Whatever is being studied, the participatory investigator has to distinguish between which parts of a description of a respondent's world are reality and which are myth. I have seen fieldwork reports, of areas that I know well, where the myth has been confused with the reality to damaging effect.

So how does one tell the difference between myth and reality? Obviously by reflecting on what one understands about a society after one has become well socialized into its ways. But surely, if one must be well socialized before one can see the difference, doesn't this lack of discernment hinder the process of becoming socialized? Of course—it is an iterative process helped by acquiring technical understanding, as discussed further in chapters 3 and 5, and by the nondeferential approach, introduced in chapter 5. What is helpful is to be well aware of, and sensitive to, the difference between myth and reality from the outset, and to bear in mind the danger of mistaking one for the other.

Explaining, Describing, and Convincing Others

Another part of sociological method is to learn how to explain what you know to others who don't know what you know, not even tacitly. That is the hardest part of all—in fact, it seems impossible in principle.

Specialist Languages

The difficulty in principle is that there is no language to bridge the gap between the researcher and audience, because part of becoming a member of a new social group is learning their language—both literally and metaphorically—and significant findings are likely to be expressed in that language, a language that is not available to the audience to whom the researcher is trying to explain things. There is no well-worked-out solution to this problem, but, in practice, the extensive use of quotations from the speech of respondents seems to transport the reader a little way into the world one is describing; this is to borrow the techniques of the novelist, at least as far as the use of speech is concerned. We'll discuss it further in chapter 8.

"Subjectivity" and "Objectivity"

As intimated, another difficulty about convincing one's audience is that the fundamental method, as described above, is in a sense "subjective": the researcher goes into the target community, becomes socialized, and then returns and tries to explain what it felt like. The word "subjective" has negative connotations in societies in which Western science is a constitutive element—it sounds like anyone could come back out of such a society with any findings that took their fancy or, at least, that their report would be subject to all manner of uncontrolled biases. That's why Gary Sanders was suspicious of my methods. Because we know how misleading subjective impressions can be, scientists invent experimental protocols, such as double-blind testing, to eliminate them; they are supposed to take the subjectivity out of the research. So what chance does an essentially subjective method have when it comes to scientific credibility in a skeptical world?

The answer is not much, but only because the relationship between subjectivity and objectivity is not well understood. First, all scientific research is subjective, because any observation, including a meter reading or the setting down of a computer output in a research report, has to be executed, in the last resort, via the senses. That means even the hardest sciences rest on the subjective, and what counts as credible depends on the community in which it is presented. Furthermore, no science can proceed without taking on trust the work of others, and there is nothing "objective" about judgments of trust. The subjectivity that runs through the natural sciences is also clear from the different statistical standards applied in different sciences as well as in the same sciences over time, while Bayesian statistics are increasingly used, inserting subjective prior expectations in the objective-looking clothing of numbers. Of course, these prior expectations have always affected the outcomes of research—no astronomer is ever going to report seeing a fire-breathing dragon in the sky! All these things mean that scientific findings emerge from a social context driven by conventional social agreements. One tries to escape some of these problems by *repeating* observations and meter readings, but it remains that the background of conventional agreements are shared by all the repeaters too.

Without subjectivity, then, there is no science—not even physics. But subjectivity plays a more central role in sociology since the very thing being investigated is mediated by the subjective—what is being investigated is the world created by the intentions of the actors in a form of life rather than a world which is supposed to be external to human action. That said, it remains that, because of the confusion over these matters, it is a good idea to try to find ways of making the outcomes of such immersions as convincing as possible to the scientifically enculturated audience.[20]

Replication

The best way to replicate a sociological experiment would be to have the experience of the immersion repeated independently by others. In the social sciences, however, this is very hard to arrange—it is so demanding of resources as to be nearly impossible and, in any case, societies can evolve between one immersion and the next. Nevertheless, if qualitative research is to deserve the label of "science" it should be conducted in such a way that it could be replicated *in principle*. One way of moving from nonreplicable to replicable (in principle) is to make sure the results are expressed at a high level of generality. When the results of a piece of fieldwork are reported as being applicable only to the local situation, then it is not science that is being done; if, however, conclusions are drawn at a level general enough for them to be compared with the outcome of a piece of fieldwork in a different location, or concerning a different group, then science is being done, and the possibility of replication is enhanced. To give an example, the experimenter's regress, described above, was initially discovered as a result of fieldwork in gravitational wave physics, but it is a finding at a general enough level to be shown to happen in parapsychology, cold fusion, and in every other controversial science; so it is a replicable and therefore manifestly "scientific" finding, even though it was discovered through the method of subjective immersion in a social collectivity along with reflective philosophical analysis. I leave it to the reader to think about the compartmentalization that goes along with supporting the finding that replicability cannot work as advertised, by citing its replicability![21]

A useful way to think about the question of how widely to generalize a finding can be found in the sociology of scientific knowledge under the heading of *evidential significance*. Solar neutrinos—neutrinos coming from the center of the Sun—were first detected by looking at the way they transmuted a few chlorine atoms in a large, underground tank of perchlorethylene cleaning-fluid into argon atoms. Pinch argued that this finding could have been presented in a number of ways, each with increasing evidential significance. One could say that the tank had a few more argon atoms in it every few weeks; one could say that some of the chlorine atoms were being transmuted; one could say that some of the chlorine atoms were being transmuted by impacts from particles; one could say that they were being transmuted by impacts from neutrinos; and one could say that they were being transmuted by impacts from neutrinos coming from the heart of the Sun.[22] The more evidential significance, the more interesting the result, and the more open to checking by other parties. After all, who else is going to be able to check and dispute the number of argon atoms in *your* underground tank—indeed, who is going to be interested in doing so? But as the significance broadens, there are more and more ways of checking—for instance, others can use their own underground tanks—so the "scientificity" of the claim gets wider at the same time.[23]

Using Numbers to Persuade

If replication is not possible, another way to render the subjective experience of immersion in a society more convincing is to find some quantitative correlate of what is being claimed; we'll discuss, in a new way, the relationship between qualitative and quantitative studies in chapter 9. Numbers have a particularly convincing appearance—though sometimes that appearance can be thoroughly misleading, as in the 2-sigma criterion used in nearly all the sciences, including the social sciences. It has been argued that cleaving ritualistically to formal methods and statistical standards is a characteristic of weak sciences, where there is disagreement and lack of authority; examples include psychology, where the standard for writing a paper is governed by strict rules, and mainstream economics, in which mathematical ingenuity and statistical analysis have become a shibboleth—more important to economists than finding out how economies really work.[24]

We can call this practice—cleaving to certain formulaic techniques and statistical procedures in the belief that doing so will produce science—*magical scientism*. Those who do not understand science think that it can be generated with rituals, and the journals are full of reports of such exercises. But interesting science is not a matter of techniques or procedures; it is always an act of creativity, which uses whatever techniques are useful in various combinations so as to generate something informative and convincing. In the social sciences, as I will argue in chapter 9, sometimes quantitative techniques will dominate and sometimes qualitative techniques will, with the quantitative playing the role of illustrative support. It is also true, as I'll argue in chapter 9, that any science that is wholly dependent on statistical analysis is at a disadvantage.

On the other hand, as someone who has conducted both quantitative and qualitative research, I can say (you'll have to be ready to believe this subjective account!) that quantitative research has a terrifying quality that is just not present in qualitative research: quantitative research means waiting for the numbers to come back from the field without any control over how they are going to turn out, and every now and again they completely confound expectations—a horrible and deeply emotional experience, or at least, that is how I've felt it. In a lifetime of qualitative research, I have never experienced the depth of despair that my much more recent experiences of quantitative research have sometimes engendered. It is true that as a qualitative researcher I have almost never found what I set out to find, but the experience is softer because one is in control of the gradually changing perspective. In both cases, the experienced researcher soon manages to turn disappointment into excitement at the novelty of a new and unexpected finding (again, see chapter 9), but in the quantitative case the initial kick in the stomach is far sharper and it took me longer to recover. It may be the researcher's terrifying lack of control over the results that contributes to the sense of objectivity that comes with numbers when they are used well.

To make the idea of interactional expertise more widely credible (chapter 4), I and my colleagues tested it quantitatively, using a technique called the Imitation Game (chapter 7). Here a member of one collectivity pretends to be a member of another while a "judge" tries to work out who is who by questioning the players (the players usually communicate via computer keyboards); one can count up how many people succeed in this or that condition or how many judges are fooled or not fooled by a performance. A revealing example of this work is an experiment that showed the blind to be more successful at pretending to be sighted than the sighted are at pretending to be blind. This fitted our hypothesis perfectly: the blind spend their lives immersed in the discourse of the sighted so should have ample opportunity to develop interactional expertise in sighted discourse, whereas the sighted in general spend much less time talking to the blind. The result—87 percent pass rate for the blind pretending to be sighted compared to 14 percent for the sighted pretending to be blind—was a great illustration of what we were arguing. But we discovered, through doing the experiments, that the balance of quantitative and qualitative is not what it is generally taken to be. Our experiments were statistically significant—we could claim that the results were not due to chance according to the statistical standards acceptable in social science—but we found that on its own the numerical result was unconvincing because of the opportunity for systematic error in the experiment. What we did find convincing was the dialogues that took place between the blind, the sighted, and the judges: by examining these dialogues we could see that the experiment was working exactly as we expected it to work. Given *that*, the numerical outcome clearly *was* a good measure and a worthwhile additional way of illustrating what was going on and a good way of convincing others. In this case, then, the certainty associated with the quantitative results was, at least for the experimenters, parasitical on the qualitative observations. Interestingly, this is also true of the first observation of a gravitational wave, where the 5-standard deviations were necessary to meet the conventional standards but the scientists themselves, and most of the wider scientific community, were much more impressed by the shape and coherence of the waveforms.[25]

To sum up, in this kind of case, numbers are being used for an illustrative rather than an exploratory purpose—similar to supporting an argument with a diagram. In such a case, the ingenuity of the quantitative researcher lies in designing and refining an experiment from which numerical results will emerge that will be convincing to others—it should, perhaps, be seen as a "demonstration."[26] The quantitative work with the blind was very difficult but worth it in the end even though we already knew the notion of interactional expertise had to be right before we generated the numbers. We'll discuss these issues in greater depth in chapter 9.

Methods Involving Numbers in a More Essential Way

Other kinds of social science use numbers not as illustrations but as analytic tools. Suppose one wants to know the proportion of right-wing people in a country; the sociologist wants a number that cannot be discovered using the methods so far discussed. For this kind of research, something like questionnaires and statistical analysis seems to be the only way. Even these, however, *rest on* the basic research method. Imagine you want to find the result about right-wingers for a country where you don't speak the language: you don't know how to ask questions! In any case, direct question such as "How right-wing are you?" are not revealing. Instead, questions such as "Do you believe that more or less money should be spent on public health?" should be asked. To invent questions that will work in the local context, the researcher must have a good understanding of the local culture. So, somewhere along the line, the researcher, or the research assistants, will need to have acquired the culture to which the questionnaire is to be applied, and this cultural understanding will have come through a process of socialization. In questionnaire research, this aspect of the process is invisible or, at least, not heavily stressed, because the researchers will often come from the place being researched and so will have acquired the relevant culture by default without noticing its foundational role in the method.

The Study of Science as the Source of Examples

Most of the examples of fieldwork presented in this book will be studies of science, but I'll try to show, wherever I can, that what I draw out from this experience applies in wider fields of sociology. The intention is to address sociological methodology in general, but mainly as illustrated by the methods of studies of science, and I apologize if, from time to time, readers will have to take the science examples and work out how they apply to their own substantive area of research for themselves. No experience-based book about methods can cover every substantive area of study, so some extrapolation is inevitable. The sociology of scientific knowledge, by the way, is about knowledge; it merely uses science as a convenient example, so the fact that the author of this book has done most of his fieldwork in the natural sciences is not hugely significant. I have tried to minimize the need for extrapolation by referring to fields like the sociology of religion and criminology wherever I can, but inevitably the examples are less rich when they don't reflect my own experience.

I am a sociologist whose foundational work is the study of the nature of knowledge, mostly using scientific knowledge as the object of study. Science has advantages for the sociologist of knowledge: scientists are generally not excessively rich and powerful and a lot of them work in universities, so they are more readily accessible than some other groups. Also, their *job* is to make new knowledge, so this makes their knowledge-making activities relatively transparent. Furthermore, they try to operate according to rules about who can participate in the making of knowledge and maintain sharp boundaries around their communities, and this again makes life easier. Consider someone whose interest is in the formation of artistic knowledge or knowledge of fashion, or political knowledge: the locus of the generation of knowledge in these cases is much more diffuse, which makes it harder to know if one has grasped what is going on. Of course, one of the aims of sociology of scientific knowledge is to show that the boundaries that science erects around itself are more permeable than scientists think; sociology of scientific knowledge reveals the ways in which political and social life in general influence what are thought to be purely "objective" scientific results—but the starting point in science is, nevertheless, clearer than it is in other cultural domains.

Another related feature of scientific knowledge is that its possessors are covetous of it and think they know who has it and who doesn't: school and university examinations are set up to test whether people have it or not. So in setting out to study scientific knowledge, the question of whether, and to what depth, one understands the "natives" has a harder edge than in most participatory studies, and this can lead, and has led, to sociologists of scientific knowledge being publicly scorned for their scientific ignorance by both scientists and philosophers, notably in a period toward the end of the 1990s known as the "science wars."[27] The possibility of public conflict encourages students of scientific knowledge to sharpen their arguments and to spend a lot of time reflecting on what they know: in the sciences, this can run from some sense of what science is all the way through to active experimentation and publication in the field in question. An example of a statement by a physicist-science warrior is the following by Alan Sokal in the scientific journal *Nature*:

Sokal says he is struck by Collins's skills in physics, but notes that such understanding would not be enough for more ambitious sociology research that attempts to probe how cultural and scientific factors shape science. "If that's your goal you need a knowledge of the field that is virtually, if not fully, at the level of researchers in the field," says Sokal. "Unless you understand the science you can't get into the theories." (Giles, 2006, p. 8)

I'll go on to show (in chapter 4) that a Sokal-type view is empirically false because, beyond a certain point, better sociology of science is not necessarily done by those who start out as scientists. Also, it is logically incoherent, because there is a division of labor in science. Thus, even within narrow specialties, anyone taking the Sokal position restricts themselves to analyzing the world of no more than the few specialist scientists who do exactly the same job as they do. In chapter 4, I'll argue the point in respect of the anthropology of boxing.

Nevertheless, this kind of disagreement is found within social studies of science itself, with a range of views in conflict all the way from "It's best to preserve your ignorance and remain a stranger," to mine, which is well toward the "Lots of technical understanding is needed" end of the spectrum, but with a nuanced understanding of what "lots of technical understanding" means. In my case, the tension between views on how much knowledge within the field is necessary has led to extensive research and analysis of the nature of expertise, which turns out to be useful for the analysis of methodology as a whole—which is, after all, about the kinds of expertise needed to understand social groups. This discussion of what it means to be socialized may be especially sharp in science, but its lessons apply all the way across the social sciences. Another, quite unexpected (in my case) advantage to studying science is that the sociologist can learn something about how sociology works by studying how science works and vice versa. We have already seen one anecdote along these lines; chapter 9 includes a new kind of examination of the relationship between qualitative and quantitative methods that has something to teach physicists as well as sociologists, and it emerges from putting together and comparing passages of science in physics and sociology that turn on the use of statistics. Sociologists might be surprised to discover that this comparison shifts the balance, on both sides, from a quantitative to qualitative approach—a totally unexpected spin-off from the sociology of science.

2   Participant Comprehension

Hints and Guidelines Extracted from Chapter 2

• When understanding by immersion, do not worry about your presence disturbing the situation being observed.

• Participant comprehension is different from unobtrusive observation.

• You are your own notebook.

• Understanding is not the same as "keeping everything straight."

• Do not confuse cultural contiguity with physical contiguity.

• Full practical participation in the activities of a group is impossible and unnecessary.

• Fieldwork is compromise rectified by honesty and integrity.

• Occasionally you may need to use the "retrospective reconstruction of method" method (RRoMM).

How Deeply to Immerse Oneself?

So you want to learn to understand a social collectivity by immersing yourself in it! The obvious question is: "How deep?" But before we get into this, a prior question comes out of the positivist tradition of the social sciences that, I find, lots of people still think is important. This question is: "Won't my very presence within the groups I am trying to understand affect what I am observing, spoiling the objectivity of my observations?" The simple answer is no—but we need to understand why. Exploring the reasons provides an opportunity to describe a delicious case study where this business of "disturbing the situation" was a central preoccupation. The case study is an old one and is fully described in a wonderful book, published in 1956, called *When Prophecy Fails*, by Leon Festinger and his colleagues.[1]

When Prophecy Fails

The Festinger team was a group of social psychologists who wanted to test their theory of *cognitive dissonance*, which has to do with the way people act when they hold two contradictory beliefs at the same time. Festinger's theory was that the disproof of a firmly held belief would actually cause its upholder to believe it more strongly than ever, even trying to recruit others into the circle of belief so as to reinforce the idea. To test the theory, the team infiltrated a millennial cult—a group who believed the world would come to an end at midnight on a specified date not far in the future; they would record what the cultists did when the world turned out not to be destroyed and see if it fitted their prediction. Note that the possibility that the world would be destroyed does not seem to have been considered—that's important.

Infiltrating what was a pretty small cult, who met in one of the member's living rooms, and hanging around until the putative date of destruction, was always going to be tedious. But, much worse, the presence of the surreptitious researchers pretending to be cult members would swell the size of the cult significantly, thus reinforcing the cult's beliefs and confounding the results of the observations: if the cult did show still stronger beliefs after (non)-destruction day, could this be a consequence of the swelling membership rather than the cognitive dissonance? It was vital that the infiltrators did as little as possible to amplify the effect of their presence, so they were instructed to say as little as possible and act as passively as they could.

We tried to be nondirective, sympathetic listeners, passive participants who were inquisitive and eager to learn whatever others might want to tell us. ... Our initial hope—to avoid any influence on the movement—turned out to be somewhat unrealistic. (Festinger et al., 1956, p. 234)

An infiltrator's refusal to lead a meeting, suggesting group meditation instead, created a silence, which then allowed a previously reticent group member to take a leading role for the first time; a researcher was asked to report what she could see when contemplating the heavens and replied "Nothing," and her words were interpreted as her having made contact with "the void." Whatever they did, the infiltrators' actions or nonactions were interpreted in ways that reinforced the cult's beliefs.

Note that Festinger et al. did not think that a solution would be for the infiltrators simply to say they were social psychologists come to see what was going to happen: they felt they had to be surreptitious. They visited the lavatory to make notes on bits of toilet paper so their record-keeping activities would not be spotted. The notes were needed to keep straight what they found to be the confusing and contradictory mélange of notions to which the cultists introduced them. They were probably right to keep their purpose secret, as the cult would probably not have welcomed observation by social psychologists at the most significant moment of their own and the entirety of humanity's lives, and maybe the presence of known social psychologists, even if they had been allowed in, would have had a still more worrying influence on the situation.

To cut a long story short, the night of the predicted catastrophe came and went without the destruction of the world, and the group members' sacrifices—giving away their possessions, cutting zips out of their trousers as metal would interfere with the process—proved in vain. Or did it? Mrs. Keech, the pseudonymous cult leader, did in fact report a few hours after the fatal moment had passed without incident that she had received a message from "Hoova," her heavenly contact, explaining that the group's faith had been enough to spare the world from destruction, and, indeed, the cultists did set out on a campaign of recruitment. Festinger and his colleagues were satisfied that they had demonstrated that their theory was right—cognitive dissonance leads to reinforcement, not disillusion. Critics, on the other hand, questioned whether any cognitive dissonance had actually occurred; the reassuring message to Mrs. Keech in the early hours of the morning was surely itself reinforcement rather than dissonance inducing, exactly analogous, as it was, to the biblical story in which Abraham's willingness to sacrifice his son, Isaac, was taken as a similar positive demonstration of faith worthy of reward. But the interpretations need not concern us, only the method and its problems.

Investigating Spoon Bending

Now we compare the millennial cult study with one where I and my colleague were faced squarely with the same question about disturbing the situation we were observing. This was in 1975 and we were observing children of around eight to ten years of age who claimed they could bend spoons by paranormal means—rubbing them between thumb and forefinger until they became soft and flexible, after the fashion of Uri Geller. We were doing a participatory study in the sociology of science, on this occasion coming close to taking a full part in the science.

I had chosen parapsychology as one of my case studies for my PhD: the others were a continuation of the TEA-laser study, which had given rise to my first published paper in 1974; gravitational wave physics, which would lead to my second publication in 1975; and the theory of amorphous semiconductors. Fortunately, or unfortunately (in some ways I might have been better off doing other things), Uri Geller appeared on the scene around this time, and a few physicists took him seriously and tried to investigate his powers. Physicist and professor John Taylor of London University said on a television show that Geller's abilities could not be explained by science, and this incident, and the overall Geller bubble, provided an opportunity for a research grant application following on from my PhD work; I was lucky enough to get the grant. One of our colleagues in the physics department of Bath University—my university—knowing of my interest in parapsychology, invited me to collaborate in his research on spoon-bending children; a host of these children had come forward claiming that they had the same powers as Geller. Naturally, I agreed—how could I not—and Trevor Pinch, who had joined the Bath team as a researcher funded by the Geller-related grant, joined in.

We entered the research with an open mind: after all, if it was good enough for some high-powered London University physicists to say the Geller phenomenon was real enough to be worth investigating, who were we to say no? Perhaps more to the point, we were working at the time with a strong relativist philosophy: my 1975 paper began with a quotation from McHugh's "On the Failure of Positivism":

We must accept that there are no adequate grounds for establishing criteria of truth except the grounds that are employed to grant or concede it—truth is conceivable only as a socially organized upshot of contingent course of linguistic, conceptual and social behaviour. (McHugh, 1971, p. 329)

Thus, we went into the experiments with a view to observing the phenomenon of paranormal spoon bending and studying what scientists made of it—how they handled the explosion of this conceptual bombshell in their cognitive lives.

Part of the discourse of the time included the idea that paranormal phenomena were "shy"—they did not show up easily under laboratory scrutiny—so we decided to help them show up by disguising the way the purported spoon-bending children were observed. This was done pretty clumsily, but it was effective. We used a psychology laboratory with a large one-way mirror in the wall. The late Brian Pamplin, the physicist, recruited a number of children through advertisements in the local papers, and we invited these children to the university and led them to the psychology laboratory, where they were seated, watched by another member of the physics department, and, seemingly, filmed by a camera on a tripod. The physicist was instructed to turn the camera away from the children if they asked not to be filmed. What the children did not know is that they were being continuously watched and filmed from behind the one-way mirror.

These experiments became very well-known internationally after an account of them was sent to the scientific journal *Nature* by Pamplin. The sociological analysis as well as the details of the procedure were written up at book length in Collins and Pinch's *Frames of Meaning*, published in 1982. But here we concentrate on one incident early in the sequence of experiments that were conducted with Pamplin.

Remember, what we set out to film was a passage of paranormal spoon bending so that we had evidence that could fulfill the breaching role in a Garfinkelian "breaching experiment" (see chapter 7) in respect of the scientific community: we wanted something that scientists would have difficulty explaining, because we wanted to see how they coped. And we already knew a lot about parapsychology and its critics—far more than Pamplin. And what we saw was Pamplin messing things up.

Pamplin sat behind the one-way mirror with myself and Pinch, controlling the real film camera with us. But when things were not going well, Pamplin had a tendency to stroll out from behind the mirror and enter the laboratory, perhaps to encourage the young subject or some such—maybe direct the dummy camera inside the laboratory away from the child. The trouble was that when he did this he tended to walk between our genuine camera on the other side of the mirror and the child-subject with her spoon. We knew, from our experience of parapsychology's critics, that if the spoon was obscured for only a moment then the critics would claim that it was at that moment that it had been bent by ordinary force, and we would have nothing with which we could confront the scientific world for the purposes of our breaching experiment. But we were supposed to be observing the situation! If we told Pamplin to stop walking into the laboratory, we would be interfering with the unfolding science. At that time we had no theories about how to do participant observation and we were beset with the idea that you should not interfere with what you were observing.

Scientific instinct came to our rescue in spite of what we had been taught, and we told Pamplin that he should not keep entering the laboratory or he would nullify the value of any scientific evidence of paranormal forces that we could gather. He desisted, and then we had to work out, given the methodological tenor of the times, why we were entitled to interfere in this blatant way. And that is how this chapter was born. This way of coming up with new methodological ideas will appear again in this book: you're doing some experiment or piece of fieldwork, the contingencies of which demand that you do something that is not methodologically "kosher" according to the received wisdom, but you know from scientific intuition that it has to be right. Later, you work out the rationale. I doubt if this way of developing ideas about method appears in any existing methods books. Let's call it the *"retrospective reconstruction of method" method* (RRoMM); it will appear again.

Incidentally, we never did produce our breaching provocation because the way Brian Pamplin wrote up what he sent to *Nature* (without asking us) was to say we had discovered how the children cheated. What they did (mostly) was to distract the internal observer's attention after the dummy camera had been turned away, bend the spoon by force, conceal the bend and then reveal it slowly when the internal observer was looking again. The trick worked pretty well, and the internal observers were convinced they'd seen something paranormal, though we on the outside were mostly concerned with suppressing our laughter. But we did manage a different kind of provocation: when scientists congratulated us on proving what they wanted to see proved—that the children were cheats—Pinch and I said that we didn't think the experiment proved anything. "After all," we said, "if you were a young child and were brought into a white-painted, breeze-block, brightly lit, mirrored, university psychology lab and told to piss into a pot while scientists who didn't believe you could do it looked on, you probably wouldn't be able to urinate; and, in any case, it was only half a dozen kids." This got the scientists really angry. But that is about the substantive result and you can read about it in the book—here we are talking about method.[2]

Positivism, Interpretivism, and Participant Comprehension

The method that was invented to excuse what we had done when we told Brian Pamplin to stop walking into the laboratory was called *participant comprehension*. Participant comprehension is different from good old participant observation. Good old participant observation is all about how you have to participate in order to get close enough to observe. An obvious way to classify types of participant observation is in terms of how close you get to the subjects—how much actual participation you do. As we can see, Festinger's study involved a lot of participation: the observers got right into the cult, pretending to be interested members, and spent their time in the living room night after night even though they tried not to say much. The difference with participant comprehension is that it focuses on the point of the participation, rather than on the need for physical proximity. And the point is not to *observe* but to *understand*. So, we told ourselves that when we told Pamplin to desist, we weren't disturbing what we were supposed to be observing but, rather, were participating in the creation of the science that we were trying to understand; and participating actively is a good way of developing an understanding.

Given that it was the mid-1970s, the contrast we drew between Festinger's study and what we were doing was cast in terms of "positivism" and "interpretivism." Festinger was trying to do something "scientific" and "objective," whereas we were trying to do something "subjective" and, I suppose, "humanistic." That contrast no longer seems right: I would now say that our study was both subjective *and* scientific, while Festinger's, purely objective though it was supposed to be, was based, in the last resort, on at least a bit of human understanding of what the observers were seeing—as is any science. That said, there was still a stark contrast between what the two projects were trying to do; it's just that it is better to avoid the old, simplistic, philosophical-sounding accusations: "you dirty positivist!" and the like.

Festinger's team was certainly not trying to understand Mrs. Keech and her band very deeply, or they would have taken their need to rush off to the lavatory to make notes so as to keep everything straight as a sign of failure. If you understand, you can keep everyone's views straight without any notes, because you have internalized the views that make the group function. Since what you are trying to do is become something like a full member of the group you are observing, if you succeed, your own internal states and ideas about what is going on is knowledge that is just as good as anything you get from the people you are watching. You don't need to rush off and make notes on lavatory paper, because you are becoming your own lavatory paper, one might say. Or if this seems too vulgar, you are becoming your own notebook.[3]

What is more, if you are trying to understand, you can't do it by minimizing interaction with the people who are the source of the understanding. Learning to understand is like learning a language: you don't try to become fluent in a language by doing as little speaking as possible, pretending you are not there and eavesdropping on the native speakers; you do it by doing as much speaking and interacting as possible. And if you are going to do as much speaking and interacting as possible, there is no point in pretending you are something other than you are: when you do a lot of speaking and interacting with others, they soon discover your identity, so surreptitiousness is not much use if you are trying to understand. In an ideal world, Festinger would have liked himself and his team to be "flies on the wall," nice and small so they could get really close without anyone noticing them. But if you want to learn to understand some initially strange society, you have to get in among them and be obtrusive, not unobtrusive. Trust has to be generated in some way so that you are accepted as part of the group; and this kind of participation is not going to be facilitated by hiding yourself away.

Table 2.1 summarizes the differences between what we'll call "unobtrusive observation"—the Festinger approach—and participant comprehension. The meaning of most of the contrasts in the table should be clear, but a few of them need further explanation: Line 1 refers to the distinction, from positivist philosophy, between the observer and the observed, while in participant comprehension the "observer" will try to become a participant and come to understand through participation and report as a native member, so that distinction is no longer clear. Line 4 refers to the disguise that an infiltrator might don *before* entering the fieldwork situation, whereas in participant comprehension the *end point* of the exercise is to become like a native member. Line 9 indicates that the pure observer never leaves their own professional community so can report back to that community in its own language, whereas the participant comprehender learns a new language, which won't be understood by home

Table 2.1
Unobtrusive and observation and participant comprehension: Differences

	Unobtrusive Observation	Participant Comprehension
1	Observer and observed distinct	Observer is a quasi or full participant
2	Don't disturb the situation	Disturb the situation as necessary
3	Participation is risky and best avoided	Participation is essential
4	Don native persona	Acquiring native ability is end point
5	Surreptitiousness is desirable	Surreptitiousness is pointless
6	Minimize interaction	Maximize interaction
7	Native beliefs likely to seem incoherent	Work to grasp coherence of beliefs
8	Detailed records essential	Detailed records not essential
9	Findings easy to present	Presentation of findings enigmatic
10	Any professional can replicate	Replication possible only by those who understand

professionals. Line 8 indicates that notes or recordings might ease this problem, but this is the subject of another chapter. Line 10 indicates that while replication is possible for both sides of the table, only those who have acquired native understanding can replicate the findings of participant comprehension.

As indicated earlier, the two ways of looking at the world imply a different relationship between sociological methods. We can make the point by considering another method called *unobtrusive measures*, which aims to understand human behavior by, say, measuring footfall in a museum by looking at the wear on floor covering or any such measure that does not require any physical contiguity with the people being studied.[4] We can now compare the three examples of research projects on the two dimensions of *physical contiguity* and *cultural contiguity*. If we compare the three cases from the point of view of physical contiguity, then the Festinger study and the spoon-bending study are similar in that they both involve a lot of physical contact with those being studied, even though the Festinger team tried to minimize social interaction. At the opposite extreme is unobtrusive measures, where no physical contact at all is required with those being studied—in the case of footfall one can wait until the museum is closed

Table 2.2
Two ways of looking at the relationship between field studies

		Physical Contiguity	
		Low	High
Cultural Contiguity	Low	Unobtrusive measures	Festinger et al. study
	High	Very difficult or impossible	Spoon-bending study

and everyone has gone home before collecting the data. But when looked at from the point of view of cultural contiguity—the extent to which the researchers wanted to come culturally close to the people being studied—the Festinger study and unobtrusive measures are in the same space while the spoon-bending study is at the other end of the spectrum. The term *participant observation* confounds these two very different approaches, and that is why it is important to replace it with *participant comprehension* when cultural contiguity is central to the method. The different ways of looking at things are shown in table 2.2.

The bottom left-hand corner invites the question of whether there can be cultural contiguity without physical contiguity. The answer is no, but physical contiguity, as we will see when we get to discussing interactional expertise, need mean only closeness to the people, not necessarily closeness to their practical activities.

Fieldwork Is Compromise

Virtually all fieldwork involves compromise. Unobtrusive measures seem like an exception when it comes to pure observation, and the kind of study where the researcher reflects on, say, a working career within the group being described is an exception at the other end; but the Festinger study involved compromise in all the ways they influenced the group, and they failed to record everything, while the spoon-bending study would have been more complete if one of us had been a working physicist before we embarked upon it. But for most field studies, the questions are "What are the compromises?" and "How damaging are they?" It is vital to know what you are trying to do if you are to understand the compromises being made, and vital to understand the compromises if you are to assess their importance and describe them in a research report. It is not all bad news by any means. Mostly, compromises are not too damaging, and illuminating fieldwork can be done under adverse circumstances and with little in the way of resources. The crucial thing is to understand the compromises, face up to them, and describe them and their consequences. Science is all about honesty and integrity; honesty and integrity are much more important than perfection.

A lot of this book will be about how to assess and analyze the compromises we need to make in fieldwork and how these consequences differ according to the aim of the research. One thing I will argue at length is that sharing the physical activities of the group being researched is far less important than it is generally made out to be. Getting involved physically is generally a good thing; it can solve problems of access, it makes the research quicker, easier, and more natural, and it tends to bring a lot of kudos to the researcher. But it is not *necessary* and it doesn't add much in terms of what can be learned. This is obvious once it has been explained, though it is little understood, and for a researcher who has gained full physical access to a field site, it is hard to admit.

Why doesn't full participation add much? Simple—at least in the case of modern societies: in modern societies there is likely to be a division of labor in the group being studied so that even the natives participate physically in only one small element of the range of physical activities. They themselves understand their fellow natives not by engaging in the same physical activities, because that would be impossible; rather, they understand them by immersion in their linguistic discourse, and such immersion will work for the sociological researcher too. All this is just as well or there could be no criminology without risking imprisonment, no study of the immensely rich without being immensely rich, no study of top-level sports without being a top-level athlete, and so on. This idea will be explained under the heading of *interactional expertise*, but the explanations of other kinds of compromise and their consequences are scattered throughout the chapters. We'll finish here by noting that what counted as a compromise for Festinger's team was quite different from what counted as a compromise in the spoon-bending study, even though our field locations were similar, because we were trying to do different things.

3 Feeling Your Way in Interview-Based Fieldwork

Hints and Guidelines Extracted from Chapter 3

• Stay light on your feet: expect plans to fail.
• Exploit respondents' social obligations if you can.
• This is what it feels like to understand nothing.
• Only understanding leads to authenticity and a lively interview because the discourse belongs to the respondent's world not the analyst's world.
• Use a tape recorder—respondents soon forget it if the talk is lively and those who don't are usually providing the myth not the truth.
• Think about this code of practice for interviews and anonymization.
• Use the left-hand page of a hardback notebook as a fallback prompt for interviews.
• Have a conversation; don't conduct an interview.
• Domain discrimination: acquiring an understanding of the reputations of scientists in a field is much harder than acquiring an understanding of the technicalities.
• The same fieldwork setting can serve different purposes: know what you are aiming for.
• How to transcribe while being careful of the pitfalls.

The TEA Laser and Tacit Knowledge

My fieldwork in science began in 1970 and, of course, I didn't really know what I was doing except that it involved the idea of form of life. In retrospect, as I will explain more carefully in chapter 11, I can see that the whole of my career has turned on that single idea. When I started my sociology degree I was always most attracted to Durkheim's sociology because it made sociology a distinct discipline: "treat social facts as things." And I was also gripped by the sociology of knowledge—the extraordinary idea that most of what you thought you believed for good reasons was actually an accident of where you were born and brought up. When I discovered that this idea could be applied to science too, my research future was fixed. Various contingencies led me to spend a lot of time trying to understand Peter Winch's book, published in 1958, *The Idea of a Social Science*—a very difficult book, which, on the face of it, was hostile to sociology, claiming it was misbegotten epistemology. Gradually I learned to understand what Winch was saying, going back to read Wittgenstein's *Philosophical Investigations*, on which Winch's book was based, and finding it easier to grasp through Winch's eyes. I was fascinated by Winch's discussion of the germ theory of disease, quoted in chapter 1, and which, in my published works, I must have quoted more times than any other passage from the literature.

My first piece of fieldwork didn't start out as anything well planned or novel; I was just looking for something to do for the dissertation that had to be tacked on to the end of my master's degree, and I knew I wanted it to be about science. My supervisor at Essex introduced me to some biologists who were looking at gels as the precursors of life, but I didn't get any sense of where it would lead. Luckily, they, in turn, introduced me to some scientists trying to build a new kind of laser, which had a good feel to it for reasons I could not entirely pin down, but the laser was small so you could "get your arms round it"; it was transparent, so you could see all its parts; it was excitingly powerful; and it was very difficult to make one work. I decided I would do a study of information transmission between laser builders, in the tradition of American work on knowledge transfer among medical doctors—the *two-step theory of communication*. But I knew I wanted to make the idea of form of life central to the project—I wanted to treat knowledge transfer not as the passing around of discrete bits of information but as the learning of a new language, like French: something that would involve immersion in the "way of being" of laser builders.

From the scientists at Essex I found out who else in the UK had built or was trying to build one of these lasers and I drove around interviewing them, growing the snowball sample as I went. I wanted to know not just where they got their information from but how they gathered it and how they learned from it: in particular, I wanted to know whether this way or that way of gaining information was better if you wanted to build one of these very recalcitrant devices and make it work. And, I was lucky—being lucky is very important in fieldwork (I recommend it)—no laser builder who obtained their information from the literature alone managed to build a working model, and every laser builder who spent time in another laboratory where the laser was working did manage to make a successful device. After a few more chance happenings, I wrote up the study as being about the importance of tacit knowledge in science (I didn't know the term *tacit knowledge* when I started). In terms of reputation it has been one of my most successful papers—a standard reference concerning tacit knowledge in science, reprinted twenty-five years later. And it all began with half a dozen interviews for a three-month dissertation.

If there is a lesson from this experience it is "Stay light on your feet." I didn't really know what I was setting out to find, but as soon as I discovered some scientists working on something that interested me I decided to stick with it. Then I found an excuse to stick with it: the knowledge transfer business. Then, when I finished, I found my project had been about something else—tacit knowledge. But all this was possible only because my fieldwork was driven by an idea, not a plan. It was driven by the idea of form of life; that told me what questions to ask, and they turned out to be good ones, even though at the outset I couldn't see exactly why they were good ones. The next project was even more bizarre, since its success was based on a disgraceful error! Even I cannot turn this into a virtue or a methodological guideline—"Try to make mistakes"—but "Stay light on your feet" is certainly relevant.[1]

An Interviewing Road Trip

The next bit of fieldwork was for my PhD at Bath University. I decided to follow up the TEA laser study and to add some other cases to it where the science was more competitive; I thought I wanted to see if competition made a difference to the way knowledge was transferred. So I picked two controversies I had read about: one was Joseph Weber's claims to have detected gravitational waves, and the other had to do with parapsychology—in particular, the claim that psychokinesis had been demonstrated using the "Schmidt quantum random number generator." I would travel north to

Figure 3.1
In Philadelphia before the cross-country trip, 1972; in a Ford Galaxy, with my friend's wife and child.

Quebec and then across America interviewing scientists involved in these fields in the same way as I had done in the UK for the TEA laser study.

My nominal supervisor was Stephen Cotgrove. I say "nominal" because it was the fashion at the time in the UK for PhD students to treat their supervisors like fools, and I was no exception. Cotgrove did make a good suggestion, however: he said that I should add a theoretical case to the other three. I chose the theory of amorphous semiconductors, around which there was a bit of a controversy too. So, with the help of friends in Philadelphia, I bought an old car and set off on a quintessential road trip, much of which was along Route 66. Stupidly, I took no photographs and kept no diary—I had some notion of pure concentration on the science—but on most evenings on the drive west I sat in some remote and very cheap motel room in my boxers, drinking Bud and watching the World Series on a black-and-white TV—this was 1972.

Nearly everyone agreed to be interviewed, but I had to work hard to persuade Joe Weber, who was, at that time, one of the busiest and most important scientists in the world. He felt his time was better spent doing physics than talking to a sociologist.[2] But because I had been careful in writing to people *not* to ask if I could interview them but only to inform them that I would telephone when I reached the United States—remember, this was before the days of email—I was able to persuade Joe Weber by talking to him on the phone: he was in Maryland and I was in Quebec, and I was promising to drive all that way just to talk to him for a half hour. One must exploit such moral obligations as one can, but one has a relatively easy time of it if one is interviewing fellow academics. I got to everyone in the end.

So here I was interviewing four sets of scientists without quite knowing why, except in the case of the TEA laser where it was a matter of filling out and completing the network of information exchange with the idea of tacit knowledge to the fore. The next-easiest group to explain were those involved in the theory of amorphous semiconductors. It was quite simple: I couldn't understand a word any of them said to me. I simply could not get my head around what they were telling me. They spoke a technical language involving something called "phonons" but I could not picture what those were (I think I might now have a slight inkling). The interviews were boring for me and, I am sure, they were boring for the physicists: each followed the same pattern—basically a half hour of the physicists explaining the theories to me while I sat there nodding in what I hoped was a way that made it seem as though something was sinking in, but I am guessing the physicists realized I was getting nothing. I kept asking them who they disagreed with and what they disagreed about, but I could not remember from one interview to the next; it was as though I were trying to learn something by rote in a foreign language; the world of the theory of amorphous semiconductors was not taking on meaning. The landscape of the field was not taking shape with details coming into clearer focus, as it should have been—a tableland of agreement here, a canyon of disagreement there; to me it was a featureless—amorphous—wasteland.

So why do I say that Cotgrove made a good suggestion, given that after about a dozen interviews I simply abandoned the whole amorphous semiconductor project? Because it was a really valuable experience. By knowing what it was *not to* understand, I came to understand what it was *to* understand. I came to realize how much, whatever it was I was doing—and mostly I still did not know—depended on understanding the domain of the science I was looking at. The question of how much science you need to understand to do the sociology of scientific knowledge has been a constant theme for me. There are those who claim you do not need to understand the science to understand it sociologically, and even that it is better not to understand the science because the perspective of the stranger is so valuable; this is a theme in ethnography in general.[3] But here I was experiencing the ultimate version of the perspective of the stranger , and it was doing nothing for me except providing an invaluable contrast with the way my other interviews were working out. I still didn't quite know what I was doing with those other interviews, but they felt absolutely right in comparison with amorphous semiconductors, which felt absolutely wrong. Regarding the need for at least a modicum of understanding if one is to get anywhere, this is the lesson of brute experience; but there may be a more theoretical argument, which we'll come to in a moment.

Some Technical Points

Recording an Interview and Maintaining a Conversation

Always record the interview—as mentioned, and I'll explain a little more fully later, respondents' quotes are a good way to tell a story. Some respondents will feel edgy when they see a voice-recorder (especially those great big tape recorders we used in the 1970s), so I always introduced the machine in terms of it saving me having to scribble lots of notes, rather than anything more important. I find that very few interviewees are bothered by the tape recorder, and for almost all of those who are, their wariness disappears after a few minutes if the interview is lively. There are just a few who, one can see, always have their interests in mind when thinking about what they should say; one can see the wheels turning in the pauses before they answer a question and the conversation never takes flight. The statements of interviewees like this are not worth much anyway, except that they provide the "myth"—which is itself useful. But one has to generate a lively conversation that leaves no time for too much thought if one is to come away with something authentic; mostly, one does not want "pat" answers—answers that are drawn from the "official" line of how scientists (or any other respondents) are "supposed" to act. One can see, once more, what a disaster the interviews were in the theory of amorphous semiconductor case, where I could not create any kind of lively talk.

Now, the "theoretical" reason for understanding as much as possible is because that is the best way to generate a lively conversation and also an authentic conversation. In engaging with respondents' technical concerns one is entering their day-to-day world, whereas if one is asking them: "How do scientists decide on this or that?," or "What do you do when you confront this kind of dilemma?," or "What is the role of graduate students in your research life?," one is asking them to enter *your* world. These are analysts' questions, the answers to which are mostly found within the body of tacit practices of scientist-respondents. As intimated in the remarks of Richard Feynman on ornithology, nothing in the professional life of scientists causes them to reflect deeply on these matters, so answers to such questions are likely to consist of some formula they have learned by rote. The job of the analyst is to find better answers to these questions, and to infer these better answers by skillful, *estranged* reflection on the life of scientists based on an understanding of that life. Talking technicalities is the best way to enter the authentic life of scientists to the point that *you* can reflect on it rather than asking the scientists to reflect on it for you; some scientists can do this brilliantly, but most cannot. I would guess that this point must apply even more so to other areas of investigation such as religion or criminology.

Code of Conduct for Interviews

Nowadays there is a great palaver about ethics in the social sciences; it seems to me we are top heavy with ethics, and it is stultifying to ask respondents to sign a permission form before they start talking to you. From the 1970s to this day I have never done this; all respondents are given is my promise not to quote them over their name without writing for permission first, and I cannot see what is wrong with this—it is much more than one gets from journalists. In later years I published on my website (see below) a "Code of Practice for Interviews," which I invited respondents to read (see appendix 1). The bottom line of the code was that I would try my hardest never to embarrass anyone with anything I quoted. This meant that sometimes when I quoted people, or paraphrased what they said, I would anonymize them. Anonymization, however, is rarely proof to the determined detective. Thus, I never promised that my recordings would be secured in a thief-proof or hacker-proof location; I explained that I did not think the stuff I was collecting deserved that exaggerated kind of security. There might be fieldwork where it is worthwhile, of course. I also explained to respondents that, as they all knew each other, and would know each other's views, it was quite likely that the source of even an anonymized quote would be evident to many of the anonymized respondent's colleagues. Anonymization only works properly with outsiders, but since insiders know what their colleagues think anyway, nothing much was being given away. Respondents saw the sense of all this, were happy with the Code of Practice, and did not demand more.

This protocol went wrong only once. This was when I sent my list of quotations to a famous scientist but, foolishly, embedded the quotations in the pages of text in which they would appear. The famous scientists decided he did not like my analysis and told me I could not use any of his quotations. I argued back telling him that I had sent the quotes to him to make sure they were accurate and that it was no more his business to censor my sociological account of the science than it was my business to tell him what he could publish and what he couldn't. But he was adamant—I could not use the quotations. So I paraphrased instead. The lesson is: send the quotes only, not your analysis. Other than that, it has been a rare occurrence for a scientist to ask me to change anything—though we will look at a revealing case in chapter 8.

Left-Hand Page

As for the conduct of the interviews, I used a technique that I still advise everyone new to fieldwork to use. I bought a hardback laboratory notebook and prepared a list of topics that would fit onto one page. These were not interview questions, but topics I wanted to cover in the conversation. I made multiple copies of the page and would glue one onto a left-hand page of the laboratory notebook for each interview. The right-hand page could then be used for notes, such as names and telephone numbers needed for building a snowball sample, jotted reminders, and so on. My interview technique was not to "interview" but to conduct an interesting conversation—a conversation interesting to the respondent as well as me (cf. amorphous semiconductors). Usually, if this was done successfully, the list of topics would be covered though usually not in the order set out on the sheet on the left-hand page—the conversation went where its logic took it, as conversations do, with me ticking off topics on the left-hand page if time allowed. But when the conversation began to run out of steam, I could check and see if anything had not been covered, and take the interview up with these remaining topics. I did have a section on my left-hand page devoted to more formal questions about who they contacted regularly to talk about their experiments, when they had last seen them, and what the contact comprised—remember, my interviews were supposed to have something to do with knowledge transfer.

Parapsychology and Gravitational Waves

There is not much to say about the 1972 parapsychology interviews except that they were a great adventure and I learned a lot about parapsychology, which would eventually contribute to some articles about the relationship between this marginalized science and the mainstream, but without much in the way of a methodological moral. What I did not know was that the parapsychology would contribute in unforeseen ways—but that was to happen sometime later. If there is one lesson to be taken from this work, and it applies to amorphous semiconductors too, it is get as much experience as you can and learn as much as you can about the broader field of your case study—in this case, science as a whole. Getting more experience cannot be planned: just follow wherever life takes you; what you learn will probably come in useful in the future even if, at the time, it is not obvious how. This is a completely different model from the carefully designed research project.

The gravitational wave interviews were going swimmingly and I was rapidly increasing my understanding of the science and its personalities and rivalries. The argument between the scientists was clear and the characters were a bit larger than life and, to my surprise and gratification, were willing to talk to me in a very frank way. I think this, once more, was luck: this fieldwork was being done in America and Americans like to talk openly; I think things would have gone far harder for me if I had been interviewing in Europe, where there is a higher proportion of people who think carefully before they say anything into a tape recorder. Here I knew that just publishing some of the colorful comments that people were offering me about other scientists' science would, by itself, provide an image of science that was very different from that of the philosophers and the received model of the time—some kind of pure, quasi-logical, stepwise set of procedures conducted by saint-like geniuses in white coats. When, in 1972, a scientist said to me of another's work, "That experiment is a bunch of shit," I knew that the sociology of science was going to change in an interesting way even if I didn't know quite how.[4] I was having fun, and I had no doubt that I was doing the right kind of thing in my interviews—whatever that thing was. Because I could build my understanding of gravitational wave physics through talking to the scientists (as with the TEA laser and parapsychology), my interviews were full of this kind of liveliness. Incidentally, I have never relied on reading the literature as a primary resource for understanding the science; rather, I use it as an initial and somewhat thin introduction to a subject so as not to seem too ignorant at the outset. Given how socialization works, this seems the right way to go.

Domain Discrimination

It has taken me a long time to grasp this, but you cannot understand a scientific controversy unless you understand the people involved, and coming to understand the people involved is much harder than coming to understand the science. *Domain-specific discrimination*, or *domain discrimination* for short, is a very recent addition to the vocabulary of expertise, emerging from our research related to what is known in science and technology studies as the "Third Wave" of science studies. This began in 2002, but the term domain-specific discrimination did not make its way into print until 2011 and I did not understand its *methodological* significance—how hard it was to grasp—until around 2016, so what is being said here is very much a retrospective analysis of something that was happening the best part of half a century earlier.[5] Of course, I did realize that scientists were telling me that some other scientist was either competent or incompetent, but this happens at two levels: there is the individual scientist's estimate of other individual scientists, and there is the general reputation of a scientist in the specialist domain that leads to that person's remarks being trusted or not trusted. What I was seeing in the 1970s was individuals' assessments of other individuals; what I was not understanding in those days was that some scientists' remarks are taken much more seriously than other scientists' remarks regardless of what they are saying, and that to understand a controversy properly you have to know different scientists' reputations.

What I now realize is that it is harder to acquire and maintain a model of who is and isn't trusted in a domain than to learn the technicalities of the domain. To learn and maintain an understanding of reputations requires extended and continuous fieldwork. What we now call "domain discrimination" is needed by scientists to find their way through a scientific controversy because it is an input into their continual assessments of the value of other scientists' work.

Learning how scientists judge other scientists, as scientists, is part of participant comprehension, at least in the case of research on science. It must also be the case in other knowledge-producing domains such as art, religion, politics, teaching, acting, and so on: one has to know the reputation of the person to understand the extent to which they are able to make a society-changing impact, and the sociology of all such domains—and there are indefinitely many—will share the problems described here. Indeed, it must be the case wherever credibility is at stake, and that is pretty well everywhere that humans interact.

I realized just how hard it is to keep abreast of the credibility of different actors only when I was writing up the final, 2015, discovery of gravitational waves. By 2015–2016, my knowledge of what was now a 1,200+ strong body of scientists had become sketchier than it was—inevitably, I knew a far smaller proportion of the actors, and was also less thoroughly immersed in the technical discussion because I was going to fewer meetings than in the 1990s. But I found my technical knowledge had eroded far less than my knowledge of the people. Furthermore, given the enormous technical knowledge I had by the 1990s (something that will be illustrated when we get to Imitation Games in chapter 7), I could catch up on anything I didn't understand with an email or a telephone call. But I could not develop an understanding of the people this way: to understand people, you have to spend time with the people who are talking about them. So, in my 2016 write-up of the discovery, every now and again I had to rely on my "native informant" for the impact of someone's reputation. Examples of my learning this kind of thing from my informant will be given in chapter 9.

The Big Mistake

Back to 1972. I've nearly completed my East–West journey and am driving through Nevada—endless scrubland. I'm thinking about how I am going to write up the gravitational wave study as a kind of more competitive version of the TEA laser study. Suddenly the hairs on the back of my neck stand up:

I can't write it up—the whole thing makes no sense at all and I have wasted my time and the Social Science Research Council's money; I'm finished as a sociologist. Nobody can be excused the terrible mistake that I've made with my careless confidence: I should have been designing and planning what I was doing all along; all those people had a reason for telling me to plan and I was too self-confident to realize that I should be taking notice of those who know better than me.

What was my mistake? Go back to the TEA laser study. A crucial feature was the difference between those who used the literature alone to gain the knowledge of how to build a TEA laser and those who spent time in someone else's laboratory. None of the former managed to build a working laser, whereas all the latter did manage it—that was one of my strokes of luck in how the fieldwork panned out. And that difference was the basis of my claims about the vital importance of the transfer of tacit knowledge. So the foundation of the whole study was my knowing whether the scientists had managed to build a working TEA laser, and it was easy to tell because the device generated a powerful beam of infrared radiation that could make concrete smoke. But when we get to gravitational waves, I don't know whether a scientist has a working gravitational wave detector or not; what counts as a working gravitational wave detector is one focus of the controversy I am looking at, so I can't say anything about the transfer of tacit knowledge. I feel sick!

I drive on through the ghastly scrubland and it takes about twenty minutes for me to realize that there is something far more exciting than a mistake going on here. If I don't know whether the scientists have a working gravitational detector, the scientists don't know either! The TEA laser scientists were never in any doubt about what a working TEA laser should do, but the very substance of the gravitational wave physicists' disagreement is what a working gravitational wave detector (of the current sensitivity) should do. Some, who agree with Joe Weber, think it should detect gravitational waves, but those who disagree with Joe Weber think a properly constructed and analyzed device of the Joe Weber type will *not* see gravitational waves. That is the story, and tacit knowledge is right at the heart of it: the scientists don't know who has built a good gravitational wave detector because conducting a good experiment requires the transfer of tacit knowledge, but tacit knowledge is invisible in its passage. Therefore, we usually test for whether an experiment is a good one by looking at its results. But here, no one can agree on what the results should be—what the results should be is the very topic of the dispute—and therefore they cannot settle the dispute just by repeating the experiment. When someone repeats the experiment and gets a negative result, it might be that the phenomenon is not there to be found, or it might be that their experimental procedure is no good; and because experiment depends on tacit knowledge we have no straightforward way to settle the issue.

The argument changes. To work out who is right about gravitational waves, scientists have known who is the best experimenter and has the best experiment: you can see right there why what we only later called domain-specific discrimination is central to science and why science is very different from how it had been previously portrayed. What had to be done to make the gravitational wave study work was to take the form of the TEA laser study and, as it were, turn it inside out, concentrating not on how people had learned to build a working device but on how they decided on what it meant for a device to work. I knew I had one of the greatest results ever in the sociology of science, and it did make me famous for a few years. Later, in the book I belatedly published in 1985, I called this phenomenon the *experimenter's regress*. That's why I said I might have been better off doing other things than looking at spoon-bending children in the mid-1970s—in some ways I might have been better off publishing the work a few years earlier as a book, but I didn't know much about how the academic world worked at the time and thought if a paper was good enough for Einstein it was good enough for me.

By the way, all the studies, apart from amorphous semiconductors, came together in the book because one could draw a contrast, not between TEA lasers and gravitational wave detection on the one hand and parapsychology on the other—which would have illustrated the standard difference between real science and fringe science—but between TEA lasers on the one hand and gravitational waves together with parapsychology on the other. In the former, we knew what a working device looked like and there was no experimenter's regress; in the latter two cases, we did not. This was how the contrast between uncontroversial science and controversial science had worked out, and it went all the way back to my choice of controversial sciences for my PhD studies, though the contrast that emerged was very different from what I had imagined it would be. It was not about information exchange but something far more exciting. This latter contrast was uncomfortable for the physical scientists, who never like to be associated with parapsychology, but it was far more interesting from the point of view of the sociology of scientific knowledge.

Interviewing as Participant Comprehension

As we saw in chapter 2, the notion of participant comprehension and its contrast with unobtrusive observation did not occur until well after the spoon-bending study, but, looking back, it is possible to see that the interviews I did on my road trip across America were somehow inspired by the comprehension idea. I think this goes back to that reading of Winch and Wittgenstein and the notion of forms of life, or social collectivities. Even though I was driving from respondent A to respondent B and talking to each of them for an hour or so before driving on, I think I knew I was trying to understand their society, not trying to gather anything like questionnaire responses. When I wrote up the study, I used the interviews to illustrate what scientists thought of each other and how those thoughts translated themselves into scientific conclusions. I was inventing, as became clear a bit later, what came to be called the *controversy study*—it is the retrospective reconstruction of method method (RRoMM), once more. In the controversy study, the population was defined by those interested in a specific scientific topic and the story was about how conclusions were reached about that topic; interest in how these things worked out drove the interviews rather than a more formal gathering of information about whom each scientist was in contact with and how often they interacted with each other. This only became seen as the controversy study method later, when others began to do what are called laboratory studies, where they spend their time in a single lab watching what people do regardless of the scientific topic and without feeling the need to travel and talk to others dealing with the same topic. The difference is that I was interested in the generation of specific bits of *scientific knowledge* whereas the lab-study people were more interested in *how scientists work*.

The methodological moral is, once more, that the method is not rigidly tied to fieldwork practice; here I was doing isolated interviews, but the method toward which I was aiming was still participant comprehension. Of course, there are better ways of doing participant comprehension; we have already seen this with the spoon-bending study and will see it in the later gravitational wave work too. Nevertheless, this was participant comprehension, even if an alien from another planet watching my behavior might not have realized it. Of course, the very same behavior could have been executed in the service of a much less interpretative study—the same road trip could have been used to gather information about these scientists rather than understanding. To repeat, I think it is vital to know what you are aiming at in these high-level theoretical and methodological respects even if you haven't planned how the investigation is going to lead to an outcome. If I'd planned more carefully, I never would have found my most important result, though—as I said—I can't really recommend messing things up as a method! Once more, the recommendation is to stay light on one's feet.

Transcription

Beware! These days, major research projects often employ people to transcribe recorded interviews, and most interview-based research projects use some kind of text-analysis software such as NVivo or ATLAS.ti. I worry that this trend takes the researcher away from the meaning of what's being transcribed. When I started, I transcribed everything myself, and I remember continually coming up with ideas and increasing my depth of understand in the course of the transcribing. As time went on, I did less and less transcribing and did it for a different purpose, but I would argue that one should do one's own transcribing until one is a very long way into a research project and a research career. Likewise, the data analysis software can take you away from meanings and push you toward seeing conversation as quantitatively analyzable. I think the software is OK if it is used to search the transcripts as they grow ever larger in number and extent. Indeed, before these commercial programs became available, I wrote my own program to search my interviews and return any paragraph that contained a word I was looking for—I used this as a way of finding illuminating quotations, a topic we will come back to. Actually, one can now do the same with a freely downloadable program called AstroGrep—very useful for searching entire hard disks for passages containing certain words. These ways of searching text do not require any precoding, which is not only time-consuming but also tends to fix ideas too soon—before full understanding has built up. Precoding makes you plant your feet too soon and too heavily.[6]

4 The Road to Interactional Expertise

Hints and Guidelines Extracted from Chapter 4

• Interactional expertise is enough for deep understanding; physical closeness or participation is necessary only to the extent that it facilitates talk.
• Division of labor and social life in general, as well as sociological method, rests on interactional expertises.
• But physical closeness makes life easier and can be exciting.
• Physical closeness becomes still less necessary once trust and understanding have developed.

Small Science to Big Science

In 1993, nearly twenty years after Joe Weber's claimed detection of gravitational waves had lost credibility, I took up a three-month fellowship at UC San Diego. Knowing Joe Weber had an office in UC Irvine, not far up the road, I telephoned him one day and arranged to drive up and talk to him. Unlike my earlier interviews, Weber was very happy to talk and we spent a pleasant day together. Weber, by this time, occupied a very different location in the world of science. In the early '70s he had been a famous professor, but by about 1975 almost no one believed his claims and many saw what he had done as a scientific scandal, so a visitor interested in his work was less unwelcome. I saw my trip as mainly a matter of curiosity—I wanted to chat with Joe Weber again eighteen years after I had last interviewed him, now that his fame had dissipated; I was curious to know what it felt like to have that happen to you.

But the Joe Weber I found was far from downhearted—he was ebullient, certain that his old ideas were on the point of being revived, and delighted with the fact that he had new supporters in Italy. As a result of that close to chance discussion, I applied for and won another grant to look at "life after death of scientific ideas" and, more to the point for this book, found my interest in gravitational waves revived. So after a while I applied for yet another grant to begin research on what was now the "big science" of interferometric gravitational wave detection. This meant I had to get to know a largely new community—and I wasn't attracted to their way of doing science: I could not get my arms around it and it seemed more bureaucratic than inspired. But it would turn out that, after some traumas, including some tense arguments with the directors of the big US project who had enough troubles of their own without me, I would learn to love it and understand it. An interesting feature of my transition from the small science to the big was that the same transition was being experienced by the community I knew. I lived through the switch with them, at the beginning feeling most sympathy with the "small scientists" and only slowly becoming persuaded by the other way of doing things. One thing keeping me going was that just about now—the early '90s—I realized that, if I was very lucky, nearly the entire history of attempts to detect gravitational waves would coincide with my career: I had begun the research fairly soon after Joe Weber made his first still-credible claims. But if what the proponents of interferometric detection were saying turned out to be true, and I was very lucky, the first detection could happen before I was too old to make sense of it. Remarkably, it would happen this way, and I was able to follow the discovery in real time and write it up. I was lucky enough to win grants from the UK Economic and Social Research Council that enabled me to follow the subject in depth from 1995 to 2009, though this agency could not see the point of the longer-term project, and after that my less intense contact with the field was indirectly supported by the US National Science Foundation.

In terms of methodology, the interest in this new work lay in the intense relationship I developed with the gravitational wave physicists involved in the big science of interferometry from about 1996 onward. Instead of just conducting a few interviews, I started to travel to all the conferences, becoming something close to a full member of the group. I became close acquaintances with many of them and friends with one or two. In particular, I met Peter Saulson in 1995 when he wrote to me having read my 1985 book, *Changing Order* (see chapter 6 for details). We became long-term friends, and he would advise me on every technical point about which I asked him. If this were anthropology I could have described him as fulfilling the role of "native informant," though I was careful to maintain good relations with many of the physicists so that I did not burden Peter too much nor wind up writing about the opinions of a single individual. The great thing Peter did, however, was to read all my drafts, line by line, including the 870-page *Gravity's Shadow* published in 2004, and the 408-page *Gravity's Kiss* published in 2017.

Interactional Expertise

The methodological story of interactional expertise begins in the late 1990s. By this time, when I attended the meetings or spent time at one of the detectors in Washington State or Louisiana, I was just one of the team and would eat my lunch and enjoy my coffee along with the scientists. I was never made to feel an outsider: if I sat at a table on my own, I would soon have company; my conversation was probably a little outside the normal run of the mill, and I have always enjoyed banter. But the thing I began to notice was that a good proportion of this casual conversation would involve physics—not me being instructed from on high, but tossing ideas back and forth: "Why not use seismic isolators on the Hanford detector?" "What are you doing about acoustic isolation?" "What do you think is the source of the extra noise that is generated by the use of power-recycling?" These were the kinds of things that the physicists would talk about among themselves, and they would talk about them just as readily to me.

It is important for nonscientists to note that conversations with physicists and between physicists are not mathematical or even overly technical; once you understand the way things hold together, you can understand what is being argued about even if they have more knowledge than you or may be able to think things through more quickly. Sometimes when I would make some positive suggestion it would turn out that it had already been discussed and the existing conclusion would be explained to me, but almost never was what I said stupid or treated as stupid. Note that this lack of mathematics characterizes even high-level physics discussion such as those that might take place in committee meetings where detector policy was being decided. Physics is a highly mathematical discipline, but the math is done outside the conference room and debating chamber and the results are nearly always describable in words or diagrams that are brought to the table to feed into the discussion.[1]

At some point it struck me as odd and interesting that I, as a nonphysicist, was holding these matter-of-fact conversations about the technicalities of physics with some of the top physicists in the world—physics is supposed to be the kind of esoteric discipline in which that kind of thing should not be possible. But I also realized it had taken me some time to reach the point where I could do this. In my earlier interviews in 1972 and 1975, I was certainly engaging in physics chat, such as presenting the views of a physicist to a technological rival. It had taken me a little while to work up to that, but I was always doing it with care—very much couching the counterview in terms not of what I thought but of what someone else had told me *they* thought. Now I was saying things about physics and asking questions in my own right and finding that they were being treated as though they were coming from another physicist, albeit one who was fairly junior; I was not, of course, expecting, or getting, any deference. I decided to give a name to this ability that I had learned: I called it *interactional expertise*. It was the expertise required to engage a technical specialist in talk about the specialism without making a significant contribution to it—which would have involved *contributory expertise*. I decided I had developed interactional expertise in gravitational wave physics, though I had no contributory expertise.

Interactional expertise, I now believe, is much more central to understanding the social world in general than was imagined at the outset. The way it was conceived in the first instance was as a rare and strange thing, belonging only to people like me who hung around with specialists without being a specialist themselves; but as time has gone on it has come to seem something that has enormously wide application and which holds the social world together. The first inkling that it had wider application was the realization that managers of large technical projects like LIGO worked almost entirely with interactional expertise. Like me, the managers, though they were accomplished scientists, were often accomplished in a different field and did not and had not made major practical contributions to the narrow specialties within the field they were now managing. Their understanding of the field they were managing, though more technically accomplished than mine, was of the same general kind. Gary Sanders, the project director of LIGO, was generous enough to acknowledge this in public when I presented the idea at a talk in Caltech and was party to the development of the idea of interactional expertise when, much later, we coauthored a paper on the topic.[2] At the time, Sanders had moved on to manage a different project—the Thirty Meter Telescope—and we talked about how he learned the relevant science and gained the respect of those scientists. In the extract from our interview below, we are talking about adaptive optics, an extremely esoteric aspect of telescope design, which involves moving the individual parts of a multisegmented mirror in such a way as to remove the "twinkle" from the stars by compensating for differential temperature changes in the atmosphere; the compensation is based on feedback from laser beams fired into the sky:

COLLINS You said something very interesting in the middle of that. You said you could not actually design the thing, but nevertheless you had the interactional expertise to sit down and argue through—

SANDERS I can sit down in a group of adaptive optics experts who will come to me and say, "Gary, you're wrong, multi-object adaptive optics will be ready at first light and it will give the following advantages"—and others will say, "No, it's multi-conjugative adaptive optics," and I can give them four reasons why we should go with multi-conjugative adaptive optics based on the kind of science we want to do, the readiness of the technical components, when we need them, and so on. And I will see as I am talking about it that the room is looking back at me and they're saying, "He does have a line, he's thought it through, and yes." But if someone said to me, "OK Sanders, we agree with you, now go and design a multi-conjugative adaptive optics system," I couldn't do it. I couldn't sit down and write out the equations—but I can draw a diagram of what each part does, where the technological readiness of each one is, what the hard parts are—I know the language. I actually feel qualified to make the decisions.[3]

The second indication that the concept had wider development was the realization that an organization like LIGO, characterized by a highly complex division of labor, was held together by interactional expertise; the scientists had to understand each other's jobs if they were to work smoothly together, but the very fact that they were specialists meant that they could not *do* each other's jobs: *they had to understand practices without practicing them*, and that applies to the division of labor in general wherever complex specialties are involved. This is managed through a shared language and interactional expertise.[4]

Methodological Consequence of the Notion of Interactional Expertise

We can draw a couple of methodological lessons here in addition to the substantive content of the idea of interactional expertise.[5]

How Much Participation Is Necessary?

It is obvious that, if scientists can and do understand practices without practicing them, social scientists can understand practices without practicing them too. As explained in chapter 2, this is a good thing in situations such as studies of criminal communities, but it tells us much more than this. As we have also explained, one can bring a participatory attitude into the research even when there is little participation—just a series of interviews—and this can make all the difference to what is taken away from the study. As the notion of interactional expertise formally points out, the way humans learn from each other is mostly via immersion in talk, and an interview, if conducted in the right way, can be the start of an immersion in talk.

In ethnography, one can gain kudos by engaging fully in the practices of the culture one is studying—just consider Loïc Wacquant's participation in Chicago's "Golden Gloves" boxing tournament. How can one not be impressed by this sociology graduate student's willingness to be smashed and bruised for years in pursuit of understanding? And there is never anything methodologically wrong with maximizing practical participation, even if it is sometimes morally wrong. But there is also nothing methodologically *necessary*. Indeed, any ethnography that takes itself logically to *depend* on full physical participation of the Wacquant type must be narrow in the extreme, because practical roles in societies are themselves narrow. Even in a traditional society, with minimal division of labor, there are still women and men, children and adults, leaders and led, and no one can be all of them, so a description of such a society has to depend for the most part on understanding at least some roles through interactional expertise. The same goes for Loïc Wacquant insofar as he wanted to describe the managers and the cornermen and the gamblers—insofar as he wanted to describe the exploiters as well as the exploited boxers.

Now, physical immersion in one of the roles pertaining to some society or subsociety is a good idea because it is a way of bringing you close not only to the role you enter but to all the other roles you want to understand. It can automatically immerse you in the linguistic discourses in which you need to be immersed in order to understand those other roles. Although, on second thought, even this may not always be true: boxing managers probably don't talk intimately to boxers about the way they exploit them; to learn about boxing management, it might be better to try to enter the

conversation as a fellow businessperson, or even as
than as a boxer.

The overall point is this: if one can learn about m
some society one is investigating via linguistic immersi
ment of interactional expertise—one can learn about *all* the
to understand in this way. And there is nothing extraordina
it this way—that is, for example, what technical managers   ..en they
learn to manage a new technical project. If they are good at it, they are
accepted by the practicing scientists as having developed the necessary
range of understandings to do the job—a job that, without a shadow of a
doubt, depends on deep technical understanding. One needs to separate
what is helpful and convenient—and some practical immersion is often
helpful and convenient—from what is *necessary*.

There is something in between taking part in the practices of a community and merely immersing oneself in the talk of a community, and this
is *physical contiguity*. There are two types of physical contiguity—closeness
to the people who make up the community and closeness to their practical activities without actually taking part in them. We can say that some
closeness to the people is *necessary* because you have to be close to talk to
people. We can say that communicating via email or the telephone or even
Skype is unlikely to do the job of building the trust that will allow the kind
of confrontational interview that is necessary for the development of full
understanding. But there is a two-stage process here: closeness is necessary
to build that kind of trust, but the more distant forms of communication
can be valuable once that closeness has been achieved.

Once more, we can see the way it works from the actions of the gravitational wave physics community. That community had to build trust and
understanding across a wide group of people, and they did it by meeting
together at many conferences and workshops per year—the conferences and
workshops that I attended during my intense period of immersion from the
mid-1990s to the late 2000s, when I would meet with the community half
a dozen times a year. But that trust, once developed, is not lost unless one
does something that will cause it to be lost, such as violating confidences.
So that meant the community, when it needed to communicate intensely
during the enormously exciting period following the discovery of September 14, 2015, could do it via email—a hundred or more mass-circulated
emails a day—and some teleconferences. I don't think the scientists were

pecting this, and I certainly wasn't, but it turned out there was no need to burn any jet fuel. Video was not used or missed, by the way. In the same way, because I was already so deeply embedded in the field, I could do my whole study of the 2015 discovery almost without leaving my study for the five months until the 2016 press conferences. The book was based largely on reading 17,000 emails, supplemented by only a few interviews, teleconferences, telephone calls, and personal emails. But, remember, my making sense of these emails depended on a huge body of prior face-to-face research that had given rise to the technical understandings, personal relationships, and the widespread trust on which it rested.

What about physical contiguity—being close to the work of the people, not just the people? If you want to be immersed in the talk, you *have* to be physically contiguous to the work. I spent a few weeks with the Italian resonant bar team in Frascati, helping out where I could, and I visited the sites of the big interferometers whenever I could—some of the conferences were held at the sites, and this was a good place to talk to people. I also watched the machines being built, which was very exciting and to some extent sociologically revealing: one could see the sheer growing physical presence of these devices bringing at least some scientists' minds around to the idea that the detectability of gravitational waves was fact, not fantasy. Obviously, I got as close as possible to the TEA laser when I helped to build one over a period of a couple of days.[6] I am always getting as close as possible and doing as much as possible. But one can see that this is a matter of helping the mind out—making things easier for the head when possible. But it cannot be a necessity, for all the reasons we have discussed: if it were a necessity one would never be able to understand what one had not seen, and even native members of a society (including the physically challenged) have to understand things that they have not seen or society would not work. Once more, interactional expertise has to be sufficient for sociological understanding, even if it is harder to acquire when not helped along by physical contiguity.

5   Comprehension, Relativism, Alternation, and Lies

Hints and Guidelines Extracted from Chapter 5

• How to think about alternation and methodological relativism.
• Expect to encounter episodes of mutual incomprehension; languages are incommensurable.
• How to alternate between worldviews by using the imagination.
• Alternating is hard.
• How do you know you are interacting well with respondents?
• How to deal with lies and the meaning of lies.
• The antiforensic principle: explore the history of cultures, not events.

Alternation and Relativism

The useful term *alternation* is found in Peter Berger's book *Invitation to Sociology*, published in 1963. (Berger's book concentrates on religion.) This is a book I must have read three times at various stages of my career, each time finding new things. Berger writes on page 65:

An individual may alternate back and forth between logically contradictory meaning systems. Each time, the meaning system he enters provides him with an interpretation of his existence and of his world, including in this interpretation an explanation of the meaning system he has abandoned.

Berger is explaining how all-encompassing the understanding of a new meaning system can be. This brings in one of the big contrasts we draw in chapter 2 between the Festinger study and the spoon-bending study; the Festinger team didn't want to get inside their subjects' worldview, whereas in the sociology of scientific knowledge and participant comprehension in general you are always trying to enter the other's domain.

That is where the infamous "relativism" comes in: if you do a thorough job of understanding, then you will be able to take seriously a view that is disbelieved by every "respectable" authority in the world. To succeed in gaining a really deep comprehension of Mrs. Keech's millennial cult, we would have had to be ready, at least in the first instance, to point out how successful they were in that their midnight vigil resulted in the saving of the world. *Look around you right now—we're still here thanks to Mrs. Keech!* The social forces to which we are exposed every day in our own society tell us that such a view is "irrational" or the like. The oxygen of rationality may be refreshing in day-to-day life, but it is poison to a sociology that starts with comprehension of unfamiliar societies. Thus, when we were examining spoon bending, among other things, we wanted to see it—the real thing—not just dismiss it by calling it impossible or "irrational." If, like so many philosophers, your first reaction is to partition the world into the rational and the irrational, you will miss most of what's going on sociologically. Relativism comes in many flavors. You can be philosophical about it and really come to believe there is nothing to base one's knowledge on except what society determines is knowledge. This is a hard position to maintain, and it is impossible to prove, or disprove it, as skeptical philosophy shows. Because it can't be proved, in 1981 I replaced it with methodological relativism, and this has remained the guiding principle for my sociology of knowledge work (but, as we will see in later chapters, not all my work).

Methodological relativism still causes a lot of fuss in studies of science. In studies of science, methodological relativism demands that the world is treated as though it in no way affects what scientists come to believe about it. It is understood best by thinking of the counterpart in studies of religion, where it is obviously the right approach. Suppose you wanted to do research on why Southern Irish Catholics believe the wine in the Mass turns into blood while Northern Irish Protestants believe it is only symbolic. The last thing you would want to bring into the explanation is the question of whether the wine *actually* turns into blood! Maybe it turns and maybe it doesn't, but you had better be a relativist about it and accept that whether it turns or not does not affect people's beliefs about whether it turns or not. That is how methodological relativism works when it comes to studies of science, too. Why, in the 1970s, did some people believe that

Joe Weber had detected gravitational waves and others believe he hadn't detected them? If you think you have to know whether he had actually detected the waves to answer that question, you are in deep trouble as a sociologist, because no one knows. You have to ignore what nature may or may not be telling Joe Weber if you want to understand the source of scientists' beliefs about what Joe Weber had found. This is the only way to push the *sociological* explanation to the limit of why this belief rather than that belief triumphed. If you think that the truth determined the belief, the exercise, in any case, is circular. The right approach is to work as though the beliefs determine what comes to count as the truth, not that the truth determines the beliefs.[1]

Alternating Can Be Hard: The Problem of Learning a New Language

Entering an unfamiliar society and learning its language can be hard, not only because the home society is always drawing you back—the swimming pool has powerful tides—but because the meaning of words can be different in different social groups. When Martin Kusch, a philosopher, and I, a sociologist, set out to write our book *The Shape of Actions*, we began with long sessions in front of a whiteboard, drawing diagrams and discussing the difficulties, but we seemed unable to understand each other. It was at least a month and probably longer before we realized that we meant radically different things by the very word on which our project turned: *action*. In philosophy, we came to realize, the idea of an action grows out of concerns to do with responsibility in courts of law: a philosopher might ask, "If the captain tripped on the ship's cat and unintentionally fell against the torpedo-firing button, so sinking another vessel, was the captain responsible for the outcome?" To a sociologist, at least one like me, that would not be an action; it would be an accident. An action would be something like divining a witch or taking out a mortgage—some typical action that contributed to the constitution of a society. Kusch and I eventually came up with the term *formative action types* to cover this meaning of action and things then went smoothly between us, so, in that case, the untranslatability was not profound. Nevertheless, it took us a long time to overcome the initial misunderstanding, because it didn't occur to us that we could be using such a central term to mean different things.

LANGUAGE	ORIGINAL	TRANSLATION	BACK TRANSLATION
Hindi	I field at short leg	शॉर्ट लेग पर मैं मैदान	I field at short leg
Afrikaans	I field at short leg	Ek gebied op kort been	I field at short leg
French	I field at short leg	Je plante à la jambe courte	I plant with short leg
Chinese simplified	I field at short leg	我在短腿	I'm on short legs
Hindi	I am a running back	मैं एक वापस चल रहा हूँ	I'm walking back
Afrikaans	I am a running back	Ek is 'n hardloop terug	I'm running back
French	I am a running back	Je suis coureur	I'm a rider
Chinese simplified	I am a running back	我是跑回	I was running back

Figure 5.1
Back translations of sports terms using Google Translate (February 2017).

We can have some fun with mutual incomprehension. In figure 5.1, some examples of sporting terminology are translated into a language other than English and then translated back again into English, using Google Translate.[2]

The term *short leg* is a fielding position in cricket; cricket is played in India and South Africa but not in France or China, hence the difference in outcome between the first two rows of the figure and the second two rows. A running back is a role in American football, which is not played in India, France, or China but (so I discovered as a result of this exercise) is known in South Africa, and hence the outcomes in the last four rows. One just cannot say "at short leg" or "a running back" in French or Chinese (or "a running back" in Hindi). This, of course, is why people talk of meaning being "lost in translation" and Britain and America being two nations "divided by a common language."

Incommensurability Found
Incommensurability is a useful term when one is thinking about alternation. It is the term Thomas Kuhn uses to characterize the relationship between

successive scientific paradigms, but, since all these things are essentially the same, the term can also be used, at least metaphorically, to describe the relationship between every kind of social collectivity.[3] Pinch and I spent a lot of time trying to bring out the incommensurability of parapsychology and the ordinary world of science, alternating our lives in the two communities. When we spent time in California among the believers in the paranormal, it became obvious to us that the physical world could not possibly be exhausted by the four known forces: it became normal for us that consciousness interacted with measurement in a strange way; it followed from quantum theory that nothing could be more ordinary than that the mind would have an effect on matter, even if it was very difficult to use controlled experiments to reveal the moments when it happened—for us the problem was with the experiments, not the world. But we also knew that, after a couple of weeks back home, all this would seem, literally, incredible—we could not hold onto both worlds at once.[4]

We also reanalyzed one session from our spoon-bending observations at Bath done with Brian Pamplin. Here the methodological lesson is the extent of reflexive determination and imagination required to adopt the incommensurable worldview while sitting in one's home laboratory. We had to make ourselves strangers in our own land by temporarily importing another land in our heads. This is important for understanding the relationship between understanding and the perspective of the stranger.

We noted that one young girl, among the half-dozen we filmed, never visibly cheated though she did bend a spoon. We also noted that we had stopped analyzing when we had found a point on the videotape where we couldn't quite see what was going on and at that point she *could have* cheated and physically bent the cutlery. Remember, we had to stop Pamplin obscuring the view of the camera because we knew that such a moment would always be taken by critics to indicate that non-paranormal bending was taking place; in stopping our analysis there, we were acting like the critics. An effort of imagination was needed to note that in a different form of life we would have taken that girl's manipulations as perfectly natural psychokinetic stuff and would have been asking why all the other children were pretending to bend the spoons by physical force when, of course, they were really distorting them with day-to-day, taken-for-granted paranormal forces—the exact complement of the critics' view. That is the crucial passage in our analysis: it shows what it means to step from one worldview into another. It shows that in one form of life, obscuring a spoon momentarily will be taken as cheating, whereas in another, the same visible behavior could be taken as acting normally.

Three Questions Set by a Mathematician

In 2004, mathematician Gabriel Stoltzenberg wrote a critically questioning (but not hostile) article about the approach being described here. My reply was called "How Do You Know You've Alternated?" Stoltzenberg wrote:

Not only do they [sociologists of science like Collins] make it seem too easy "to take on the ways of being in the world that are characteristic of the groups they study," but they also fail to explain how they know when they have gotten it right. Nor do they say whether, when they "return home," they have any better luck communicating their findings than did Square, upon his return to Flatland from Spaceland. (Stoltzenberg, 2004, p. 86)

All three elements of Stoltzenberg's challenge were good ones, and we'll get back to the third one, "How do you explain what you've found out if it involves immersion in a radically alien culture?," in chapter 8. As for how one takes on other ways of being in the world, that is what most of the discussion has been about so far—for instance, do you need to practice to understand new practices? But now we'll look at the question of how you know you have succeeded when talking to scientists, assuming that something similar will apply to other areas of sociological research. I can't improve on what I wrote in 2004:

As a sociologist of science you essay research on a new specialism and you initially understand neither the banter nor the technical terms. After a painful period, if you are lucky you begin to pick up on the inferences in others' conversations and eventually you begin to be able to join in. One day a respondent might say in response to one of your technical queries "I had not thought about that," and pause before giving you an answer. When this level is reached respondents will start to be happy to talk to you about physics and even respond generously, and with consideration, to your critical comments. Eventually people will become interested in what you know, not as a scientist in your own right, but as a person who is able to convey the scientific thoughts and activities of others. If you've just come from visiting scientist X you may be able to tell scientist Y something of the science that X is doing. ... What were once "interviews" then become "conversations" that can be interesting and occasionally even useful to both parties. What also happens in a conversation is that by occasionally anticipating a point your partner is about to make you can speed things along. You might also verbally fill in some gaps that might otherwise be forgotten. You can recognize jokes, irony and when you are having your leg pulled (though, in the nature of things, interactional competence does not allow you to recognize lies). When you get good at it you can even take the devil's advocate position in respect of some scientific controversy and maintain it well enough to make your conversational partner think hard. (Collins, 2004b, p. 104)

Notice the importance of understanding jokes, leg-pulls, and banter.

Once more, this reflects the way scientists themselves learn to understand their world. Once they have passed through their formal education and entered the professional world, they will have to start to take an interactive part in discussions, asking challenging questions and putting forward challenging ideas. Deference will have to give way to banter and mild confrontation—forceful engagement with the knowledge, sometimes through argument. This is what the social scientist who wants to understand has to learn to do, and the quickest way to do it is to take the ideas of one scientist and present them to another—not as your own ideas, or you'll soon be found out—but as the challenging ideas of someone else.

In all areas of social life, to learn from immersion one must always be engaging, and engaging involves a degree of challenge. I suspect that in science, challenge comes more naturally because debate and "organized skepticism" are constitutive features of the scientific form of life. I once had a half-hour or more of heated debate with Barry Barish, the director of LIGO, over whether the project was ready to move from the development of prototypes to the building of a full-scale, one-hundred-million-dollar machine. He had decided it was ready. Taking a devil's advocate position, I told him he was wrong and stuck to my point through a whole series of rebuttals and counter-rebuttals. I cannot imagine an interviewer in a high-powered business setting getting away with anything like this; in most nonscience settings I would imagine this kind of extended argument would be thought inappropriate or even rude, not to mention a waste of time. For me it was a valuable experiment in how far one can go with interactional expertise while at the same time revealing something about the democratic heart of physics—Barish wanted to win through argument, not through authority, even when his opponent was a scientific pipsqueak like me. Incidentally, I thought I held my ground quite successfully and, for me, the argument was a draw at worst. But Barish's job was to decide what to do, and he decided to build the big machines in spite of my arguments. He, of course, turned out to be right, and that is why it was a good thing that he was the director—and now Nobel Laureate—and I was the pipsqueak.

I well remember another instance of technological interchange—not a particularly challenging one, but a useful one for the scientist and for understanding interactional expertise. In December 2002 I had been to visit the small Japanese interferometer in Tokyo, which was not working terribly well, being beset by unknown noise, as all the early interferometers were. It was widely believed that the trouble with the Japanese device was that there was stray light bouncing off the walls of the beam tubes and finding its way back to the sensors that controlled the mirrors, causing them to move in unintended ways. While at the site, I put this to my host, but he told me this widespread impression was wrong and he demonstrated it in a simple way. As we watched the interferometer output trace, he struck the beam tube with his fist and there was no jitter in the output; if light had been striking the beam tube walls, the vibration would have shown up instantly in the output. As I recall, he invited me to try it too. When I later met Gary Sanders at a conference in Kyoto, he told me in the course of conversation about the stray-light troubles in the Japanese device, but I was able to tell him he was wrong. And I could walk him through what I had seen because I understood the technology well enough to understand the demonstration. That I understood was evident from my description; Gary could tell that, even though I was not a physicist, I understood the world of gravitational wave physics well enough not to have got this wrong. So Gary's understanding of the Japanese interferometer was corrected by a sociologist—a nice demonstration of the workings of interactional expertise. Thus, it is not that hard to know when you have alternated—when you have grasped another form of life—especially if you have the experience of completely failing to grasp it, as was the case for me regarding the theory of amorphous semiconductors. You show you have grasped it by engaging with the members of the form of life: the contrast between the gravitational wave study and the amorphous semiconductor study could not have been greater.

The Meaning of Lies and the Antiforensic Principle

As I wrote in the extract above, "in the nature of things, interactional competence does not allow you to recognize lies." What I meant by "in the nature of things" is that even in your own society—the society in respect of which you have maximal cultural competence—you cannot recognize lies when they are told by a good liar—which is why we call them "good liars." If you cannot recognize good lies in your own society, there is no reason to expect to be able to recognize them in a society you are only learning to understand.

Actually, this isn't quite true; you can recognize respondents who are doing too much thinking before they answer—I have already recommended that their responses be discarded. Perhaps, though, it is harsh to call them liars; they are being judicious. There are many roles in life that call upon people to speak judiciously, and they are not generally condemned for it, or referred to as liars.

Let's get back to good old-fashioned skillful lies and lying. You cannot recognize lying; so doesn't this make all the talk-based fieldwork futile or unreliable? The answer is no because of the skill needed to tell a good lie. A good lie has to make sense. If it makes sense, then it reflects what makes sense in the society, and that is what understanding is about—coming to know what makes sense in this or that society. I still like the example I used in "The Meaning of Lies," published in 1983, and I will adapt it here only slightly.

Imagine you are an anthropologist from another planet, watching a ballroom dancing competition in that area of the British city of Birmingham called Selly Oak (a purely arbitrary choice of location, but Brits—and Brits alone—will understand its slightly humorous suburban connotations). You are watching the dance competition from the balcony, and you have with you three native informants. You are witnessing, though you don't know it, a man and a woman dancing a tango. You ask your native informants what the couple are doing. The three informants give different answers: (i) they are trying to win the Selly Oak Latin American ballroom dancing competition; (ii) they are each married to someone else but are seeking a surreptitious sexual frisson from their dance partner; (iii) they are trying to bring on rain by doing a rain dance. What is the crucial thing about the contribution of those answers to your developing understanding of Selly Oak society? The crucial thing is that the third one is a joke. No one in Selly Oak tries to bring on rain through ballroom dancing. So long as you think that answer (iii) is a possibility, you have not understood Selly Oak.

On the other hand, you do not need to know whether answers (i) and (ii) are true: they could both be true, only one of them could be true, or they could both be lies, but it does not matter. If either or both of them are lies, they are good lies, so the fact that either of them *could be* true is telling you as much about the way Selly Oak society works as if they were true. So, when it comes to understanding a society, good lies have as much meaning as truths!

I was once told a good old-fashioned lie by a respondent, but it was not a good lie—at least, not good enough to take me in. I understood enough about the society I was exploring by then to recognize that the respondent had told me a lie, and this respondent didn't realize that I understood too much to be taken in by it. It had to do with a $10,000 grant given to Joe Weber, the pioneer of gravitational wave detection research, whose credibility had pretty well disappeared by 1975. The grant was to enable him to look for a relationship between his old pre-1975 claims and what was at the time an astrophysical mystery: gamma-ray bursts. In the early 1990s, Weber was funded by NASA Goddard to search for a correlation between the two. I conducted an interview at Goddard and I asked the principal person involved about the process by which Weber was awarded the grant. He told me that it was a result of the normal peer review process. I said I did not believe that could be true because I knew that, by then, a proposal of this kind by Weber would not be seen to have credibility by a regular selection of reviewers. My interviewee then changed his story, telling me it was not a regular panel of peer reviewers but a specially selected group who were more likely to be favorable to Weber. That seemed reasonable to me, and I was happy that my understanding had stood up against the deceitful account I had been given. On the way out of the building, however, I passed the office door of another well-known party to these events at Goddard and I knocked on the door. The door was opened, and I had a friendly chat in which I was given yet another account of the award of the grant: the original party was much more directly involved as a sponsor. I was not surprised, except by the level of deliberate deceit—which is unusual in my domain of fieldwork.

Here, then, we have an actual occurrence that is parallel to the Selly Oak thought experiment: there are three accounts, two of which are plausible and one of which is not, so long as you understand enough at the outset. One can see that as far as my understanding of Weber's relationship with the scientific community is concerned—something that was an important component in my participatory understanding of the community as a whole—either of the second two accounts is good enough to reinforce the understanding. This was also nicely reinforced by my recognizing the first lie and confronting my respondent with it. That I was initially fooled by the second lie was not important, since the second lie fitted the kind of understanding I needed.

What was the added value of the second interview, which revealed that the second account was a lie too? It was extremely valuable to my understanding of methodology, and here I am writing it up in a methodology book. But I don't think it added anything to my understanding of the gravitational wave physics community, and I never wrote up the incident as part of the story of gravitational waves, even though, on many occasions, I have used the example of Weber's work on the relationship between gravitational waves and gamma-ray bursts to illustrate loss of credibility. As far as the main theme of my studies was concerned, my discovery of the second lie was a lucky contingency.

The Antiforensic Principle

This leads us to another important principle: the *antiforensic principle*. It's a principle I have drawn on over and over again when faced by certain kinds of fieldwork choices or analytic dilemmas. The antiforensic principle begins with the understanding that, in doing participatory comprehension, one's job is not to act like a detective, or a judge in a court of law, or a psychologist, or fulfill any of the other professional roles that are primarily concerned with internal states of individuals or the detailed facts of the matter. What you have to be concerned with in participatory comprehension is not what *did* happen but what *plausibly could have happened*; it is not difficult to see how this follows from the meaning of lies.

The example I use is events at Caltech around the immensely traumatic falling out of Robbie Vogt, at that time director of LIGO, and Ron Drever, the project's infuriatingly awkward genius; it is written up in *Gravity's Shadow*, listed as 2004a in the references. Vogt, driven to distraction

by Drever, threw him out of the project and banned him from the installation. At the height of this row, Drever found himself locked out of his
office—one account being that Vogt had given instructions to have the lock
changed to inflict his anger on Drever, and another account being that the
lock was changed as a result of routine maintenance and that Drever was
speedily given a new key. I spent a lot of time on the Caltech campus and
could have found the truth of the matter by talking to the building maintenance department or some such. (Though I was talking to both Vogt and
Drever about the events, this is not the kind of thing where I could have
got a story one could rely on from either of them—unless Vogt told me he
had done it deliberately—but it didn't occur to me at the time that this
was something I could ask him.) I thought about it and decided it would
be wrong to pursue the investigation, because to do so would be to betray
my methodology. It didn't matter to me whether Drever had been deliberately or accidentally locked out of his office; what mattered was that the
story that he had been deliberately locked out was abroad, and that told
me all I needed to know about what was going on in the local community.
If the relations between Vogt and Drever had not broken down so drasti-
cally, no one would have repeated such a story because it would have been
too implausible. That incident led to my coming up with the antiforensic
principle.

That incident is also the source of my understanding of why, in spite of
the fact that my books on gravitational waves are the best historical sources
in respect of many of the events from the early 1970s onward, history, in its
regular sense, is not the primary concern. If I had been a regular historian,
I would have thought it essential to track down what actually happened
and put everyone right who was wrong. But the history I most want to
get right is of the changing *culture* of gravitational wave physics over forty
or so years, not of the events; the events are a scaffold. I do record many
of the events in what I hope is—and what seems to be, from the way the
record is used by others—a reasonably accurate way. I try to make clear
how sure I am about various facts—a good rule is always do your best at
whatever you find yourself doing. But this history, however useful it is, is
a spin-off from the other kind of exploration. And this explains why my
research stresses talk, not documents. There is nothing antihistorical about
what is being said here; it is just a gentle guideline about how to distribute
the always-scarce resource of time if you are forced to make a choice. The

downside is that, for example, one of my most historical papers, as I saw it, was rejected from the first history of science journal I sent it to because "the footnotes weren't good enough" (the second history journal to which I sent it accepted it). The antiforensic principle can be a useful guide when applying for research grants—what is it that you really want to spend your time doing if you get the money? When time is short, it might also prevent you being sidetracked into some intriguing, detective-like investigation, mistakenly thinking it's sociology.

6 More on the Nature of Sociology

Hints and Guidelines Extracted from Chapter 6

- Use the distinction between actors' and analysts' categories.
- Are you really using actors' categories if actors think your analysis is wrong?
- Handle disagreements with honesty: how to use a website.
- Explaining your subject to others also reveals it to you.
  - The idea of "socialness" was discovered through explaining sociology to others.
- How to alternate between relativism and applied metasociology.

Actors' and Analysts' Categories

In the natural or life sciences, the objects that are found in the world—quarks, neutrinos, cells, mitochondria, insects, and at least the lower animals—are defined, demarcated, and classified by the analysts and the analysts alone: the natural scientists. Mortgages, witches, and such myriad other objects that order the lives of groups exhibiting cultural differences are, in contrast, defined, demarcated, and classified by the actors whose ways of living create the forms of life that give them their shape and existence—the actors who are the subject of study of the social scientists. Natural and life scientists have only one set of classifications to contend with—that established within their own scientific forms of life—*analysts' categories*; social scientists have two sets to contend with—their own analysts' categories and the *actors' categories* belonging to those they study.[1]

Sociological analysis, however, even when it starts with actors' categories, as I believe it must, does not finish with them or it would have little evidential significance. Something has to be built on top of the painfully acquired actors' perspective, and this is the creative analysts' perspective.[2]

There is, alas, a complication that does not seem to receive much attention.[3] It is especially noticeable in sociology of science, but it must show itself in other areas of sociology too. Sometimes there is outright disagreement between actors and analysts—the actors say that the analysts have got it wrong, perhaps because the analysts have not fully understood the actors. If there is disagreement, how can it be said that the analyst is basing the analysis in actors' categories? In the sociology of religion, I imagine the analysts simply have to ignore what actors say about belief being caused by revelation, or the like, rather than the social; they must act according to the equivalent of the sociologist of science's "relativism."

Here are a couple of illustrative examples of how, at certain times, the gravitational wave scientists and I disagreed on this point:

> I do not consider you "a trained observer of human behavior," so far as concerns the gravity wave field. Science and technology move ahead through advances in instrumentation and publication of results. Not through gossip or "science wars" or deep introspection about what the other guy is thinking or what one is thinking oneself.

That comment was emailed to me in 2001, by a very senior scientist (and an advisor to US presidents).

Earlier, in 1995, as a result of a similar mismatch of viewpoints, I met another of the gravitational wave scientists whom I had not heard of up until then, Peter Saulson, who would later become my friend and what anthropologists would call my "native informant." The meeting arose out of an unsolicited letter he wrote to me after reading my book, *Changing Order*. A passage from his letter is shown in figure 6.1; the relevant part of my reply is shown in figure 6.2. As we can see, this exchange reflects the argument discussed earlier in this book about the difference between the myth and the deeper reality that the sociologist has to pull out through fieldwork.

Saulson has been an enormously valuable "informant" in part because, unusually for a physical scientist, he knew some sociology at the outset and soon came to understand what I was trying to do. Once or twice Saulson even offered some serious sociological criticism, and I learned to think about my project more deeply as a result of these exchanges. These exchanges, nevertheless, illustrate radical alternation, for it seems impossible to believe both

There was one aspect of your book that left me somewhat puzzled. Since your main aim is to investigate how scientists draw conclusions from experiments, I am surprised that you do not devote more attention to how scientists think they do so. Your chapter on the TEA laser was very nicely done, but I think you've only scratched the surface. I would have expected to see a discussion of Occam's Razor, the idea that parsimony is beautiful and is therefore a guide to truth, as well as of the belief that there is a logical coherence to nature. This last belief is of course what is responsible for the conservatism of science that makes it so resistant to claims such as Weber's and those of parapsychologists. Even if it is true that these beliefs of working scientists have philosophical problems, it still would help in understanding what happens to know what the actors think is happening.

A description of the functioning of science without a concentration on the shared ideology of scientists seems ghostly and unsatisfying. Science is justified by a serious intellectual purpose. Furthermore, the institution has built in the mechanism for its own revision, the appeal to experimental tests. You have pointed out quite clearly and constructively the difficulty of applying this mechanism. I am only urging you to contemplate in richer detail the way scientists themselves grapple with the difficulties.

Figure 6.1
Extract from a 1995 letter from Peter Saulson.

```
        Second, you ask why I do not deal with scientists' own views
of what they are doing.  This is simply because they are so well
known as not to need mentioning.  There is a whole industry of
historians and philosophers of science who have created
disciplines by systematically reflecting what scientists believe
they are doing.  Work like mine is intended to be a counter to
this.  Let me say straight away that I believe that what
scientists think they are doing is extremely important for science
and scientists; I would not want my work to change the attitude of
scientists at the laboratory bench one bit.  What is more, when I
do my own work I do it with the official ideology of science in
mind.  That is, I claim that what I say is right because I have
made accurate observations, and that anyone could repeat these
observations if they looked carefully enough.  The implications of
```

Figure 6.2
Extract from my 1995 reply to Saulson.

that one is discovering true features of the physical or social world while at the same time socially constructing them—neither of us could hold on to the two views of the world at the one time; we had to switch between them depending on what we were trying to achieve.[4]

These physicists, I found, were driven by strong academic values, and this meant they were willing to tolerate me in spite of my more "philosoph-ical" writings. So the disagreements set out above took place in a context of a shared world "higher up the fractal." The idea of science, which meant different things for me and the scientists, is embedded within the idea of what it is to be an academic, which meant the same for both of us.

If there is no mutual understanding and respect of this kind, how can one respond to a clash between actors' and analysts' views of the world when one claims one is building on actors' categories? The answer is that the analyst has to believe that his or her categories are superior to actors' categories even though they are based on them—at least superior in respect of sociological understanding. One way to handle the conflict is compartmentalization: keep the analyst's world separate from that of the actors if it can be managed. But this is a fragile and not very satisfactory solution. Another way forward is the in-principle claim that, given enough time, one could reveal to the actors that though they believe their world is exhausted by their view of it, there is a deeper and more complete picture enriched by sociological insights. I cannot see this cutting much ice in the sociology of religion, but criminologists seem to have had some success in convincing those running the criminal justice system that placing certain types of criminal into "total institutions" works more to train them to be better criminals rather than to deter them. Sociology of science is an area where there is some hope. Crucially, if acceptance is to be a possibility, the deeper explanation would have to be *compatible with* the actors' world as they formerly understood it—but this is what building on actors' categories implies. To say to a scientist actor, "Your experimental results are actually determined by the machinations of witches," would not have much success; to say, "What you count as an experimental result is a matter of what your group comes to agree on as the set of the experiments that were competently performed, and this depends, in part, on your judgments about the scientists, not just your judgments about the science," has a chance of being accepted by the actors after a period of reflection.

Another implication of this model is that the borderline between actors' and analysts' categories can change if you can persuade actors that you, the analyst, has it right. One indicator of successful sociological work is such change. My analyst's category, the experimenter's regress, was built on the actors' world but was not a self-conscious part of the actors' world. But I hope that the idea of the experimenter's regress will become more widely understood by actors and become part of their world, so long as it does not do it too much damage to the way science is done, that world depending on the idea of replicability as it does. I do think that some of what I have come up with in my long study of gravitational wave physics has changed the way the physicists understand their world, if only in a marginal way.

Socialness and Sociology

Compartmentalization is not going to work as a way of handling disagreements over the long term, and it may be that in your area of fieldwork you are not lucky enough to find an overarching culture that enables the work to continue in spite of friction. Another way of handling disagreements that I found useful was building a website that described my project with as much honesty as I could muster, including an explanation of my relativist position. This website helped a lot in making my strange worldview acceptable to the scientists: they could appreciate where I was coming from even if they did not agree with the position I was advancing. I hope this is not just the luck that comes with working with scientists and that it might work in other areas of investigation, though there are obviously some in which it would be hopeless.

Putting up this website also had an important consequence for my view of the sociological world. One part of the website involved my explaining to the physicists what sociology was. As mentioned in the introductory chapter, I described the sciences according to their "fundamental units of investigation":

Physics begins with the smallest things—quarks or strings; chemistry builds upward from quantum states; biochemistry starts with molecules; biology starts with cells; medicine starts with organs; psychology begins with the behavior of entire, usually human, organisms; social psychology investigates the interaction between human organisms; but sociology starts with collectivities of humans.

Having to explain what sociology was to scientist-outsiders in a way that would make sense to them and convince them that I was doing something interesting helped me to understand the subject better myself. I think every sociologist ought to be ready to think about how they would explain their subject to others—it is an interesting and revealing exercise.

In my case, it gave rise to the concept of *socialness* that I mentioned in the introductory chapter.

"Socialness is the capacity to attain social fluency in one or more cultures." If one has social fluency one has social capabilities and one can follow rules in the Wittgensteinian sense. Which is to say that socialness, once cashed out into social fluency, enables one to carry out polimorphic actions. (Collins, 1998, p. 497)[5]

Socialness is, then, the ability collectively to form, take part in, and be constituted by forms of life. The idea can be used in three ways. One can explore the very nature of socialness in a philosophical way—we can call this *metasociology*. One can simply look at the different ways societies exhibit their socialness—this is standard sociology. But one can also ask the question: What can entities with socialness do that entities without socialness cannot do? This level—*applied metasociology*—has enormous potential but has been largely ignored. There is a parallel with the analysis of language, though "parallel" is too weak a term as language is so central to culture and therefore to sociology and metasociology. Thus, we can think about the nature of language, we can look at the substance of different languages, and we can look at what entities with language can do that entities without language cannot do—which is pretty well the same as doing applied metasociology.

Applied Metasociology and the Study of Artificial Intelligence: Methodological Alternation

Applied metasociology, of which, as far as I can see, there is either none or hardly any, is what most obviously makes sociology a distinct and unique science and humans a distinct and unique species. In retrospect—more RRoMM—it is what I am doing in my work on artificial intelligence. This work is philosophically and methodologically very different from my work on the sociology of knowledge, which has to endorse methodological relativism. In the case of the AI work, the relativism is taken to have served its purpose in helping researchers to understand what knowledge is and how it is made. By taking a relativistic attitude, sociologists have become experts on knowledge, in particular its social foundations; now that expertise is being put to use in a different kind of science. This requires the sociologist to adopt the "natural attitude" of the natural scientist. In the work on artificial intelligence, scientists and engineers are being told that their intelligent machines will not work as they think they will because they have failed to understand the social nature of knowledge.

It is just like ordinary science except that it turns on sociology's unique understanding that comes out of applied metasociology. So this is another kind of alternation—not alternation between the worldviews of respondents but alternation between methodological approaches—*methodological alternation*.

It may seem strange that I criticize scientists and engineers in AI while understanding far less of their subject than I do of the studies of parapsychologists and gravitational wave physicists, whom I do not criticize. How can this be? At the time of writing I have recently completed the manuscript of a third book on artificial intelligence, which is focused on the so-called singularity and, more generally, on deep learning and its successes and limitations. An anonymous reader who commented on the first submitted draft of the book complained that my technical descriptions of how aspects of AI worked, including my description of deep learning itself, were inadequate. As someone whose books on gravitational wave physics are full of technical descriptions of how the science works, descriptions that have been tested against the expertise of the scientists themselves, I was concerned. My 1990s books on AI had a superficial presentation of some AI techniques: for example, I painfully taught myself the computer language PROLOG and, with the help of a technician in Bath's physics department and some computing help from a friend in the Management School, I wrote a small AI program to teach people how to grow semiconductor crystals.[6] This went down very well with AI-savvy readers of the book, even though my understanding of AI was technically shallow. But this third book did not reach even that level of technical proficiency. Crucially, I knew I would come nowhere near passing an Imitation Game (chapter 7) with deep-learning AI as the target expertise.

Faced with this much more recent criticism of my lack of technical knowledge of AI, I was forced to admit that in terms of my general position about the need to understand one's respondents—the position advanced in this book—there was a problem. But, after some thought—RRoMM once more—my conclusion was that I ought to strip out still more of the technical description from the manuscript rather than add to it; this would make it plain that that no part of the warrant for the book was a deep understanding of the technicalities of this kind of AI. I do understand the principles of deep learning, and my "just so story" describing how it works has been commended by one AI expert, but I need only enough understanding to see why it is important, how it comes closer to socialization than previous generations of intelligent computers (which explains its successes), and what its remaining limitations are. This is quite different from the warrant for my work in gravitational wave physics and parapsychology. The warrant for my work in AI is not a deep understanding of AI techniques but a deep understanding of the nature of knowledge that comes out of sociology of knowledge studies. If my work on AI is worth anything, it is the applied metasociology that makes it so. It is my understanding of "what entities who possess socialness can do and what entities without socialness cannot do" that is important.

Some of what seemed impossible for the AI of the 1990s has come to pass with deep learning. Deep learning puts machines in touch with everything on the web and potentially in touch with everything that is ever written or said by everyone in the world. It is the application of deep learning to huge corpuses of human speech and writing that has led to the marked improvement by speech recognizers such as Siri and applications such as Google Translate. The subject of the recent book is the significant difference that makes to my earlier critiques.[7] The argument of the book is that deep learning has not solved the problem of socialness—and there are some very simple tricks that can show that this is so—though it has brought machines much closer to being socialized than ever before.

What I argue is that machines will not be able to do what humans can do until they possess socialness, and socialness is such an unexplored property that we won't know how to make such machines in the foreseeable future. That is why, though the AI research depends on the idea of form of life just as much as the other case studies, it does not depend on socialization into the community of AI practitioners but only an understanding of the principles of their work: uniquely among the projects reported here, it does not rest on deep participant comprehension of the work of the group being described and cannot involve a relativistic attitude to that work.

That applied metasociology does work in the AI case is made evident by the favorable reception of the early AI studies by the AI community (e.g., a prize for technical merit for a paper presented at one of their meetings and, more recently, fulsome appreciation by the software-testing community).[8] And the latest book manuscript has been favorably received and commented on by a number of AI specialists. Compare this with my attempts to say something about physics to physicists: these are nearly always treated as an amusing diversion at best—like a dog walking on its hind legs. (The one or two occasions when I have been proved right are exceptional.) So the difference between these two kinds of case study is marked even though they both rest on the idea of a form of life.[9]

To repeat, the other marked difference is that I was never telling parapsychologists, or seriously telling physicists, about the limitations of the substance of their work, whereas in the case of AI I was criticizing substantive claims. The fact that we took the actors' perspective and didn't say this kind of thing in the other case studies, and would not have even if we were studying something like Mrs. Keech's world, was iconic of just what the sociology of scientific knowledge was about, namely *symmetry*—treating what actors count as true and false equally from the point of view of social causality.[10]

The Study of Expertise and Relativism

Since the early 2000s I have been doing lots of work on expertise, treating it not as a social construct but as a product of socialization in expert communities. In retrospect, this kind of realist approach to expertise was present from day one of my research on tacit knowledge. One can treat the attribution of tacit knowledge as a social construct, but this is relatively unininteresting compared to treating it as something real; and, ironically, the idea of tacit knowledge is the foundation of the experimenter's regress. So, the work on tacit knowledge and on expertise is another place where methodological relativism is abandoned and replaced by what we can call applied metasociology: if the key is socialization into expert groups, then what we are invoking to explain the world is the idea of the social. Note again how this contrasts with any less social model of expertise—it is essentially human centered.

7   The Stranger, Estrangement, and Estrangement Techniques

Hints and Guidelines Extracted from Chapter 7
- Estrangement is what is important, not being a stranger.
- Estrangement techniques include:
  - drugs, sociology of knowledge, philosophy, and the like;
  - breaching experiments;
  - the proxy stranger method;
  - the controversy study;
  - Imitation Games.
- Imitation Games can be applied as an actual or thought experiment.
- Even the large-scale Imitation Game requires social understanding if you are to trust the numbers.

The Stranger's Perspective and Estrangement

Anthropologists and ethnographers seem to give a lot of weight to the advantages of being a stranger. By contrast, in this book I have argued that, other things being equal, one should strive to be as much like a native member as possible if one wants to understand native members. Bruno Latour, the famous anthropologist/philosopher of science with a humanist leaning, tried to illustrate the value of the stranger's perspective by showing, in his book about the Salk Institute, a photograph of the chimneys on the roof of the building: "This," he explained, "is an observation of the kind I am making of this laboratory and I need no more understanding of the science than I needed to take this photograph." But in spite of the flourish, no one ever learned anything from the photograph of the rooftop, and what they did learn about science from the book came from what he and his coauthor did eventually understand about the science, even though they tried to pass themselves off as knowing nothing.[1] In the study of science, becoming a member of the society being investigated means learning something of their science, but even I have argued that I needed less of it in my AI work than in my other studies. This is because, in that work, I am not trying to understand so as to describe and explain, but to bring a new kind of knowledge—an understanding of the social nature of knowledge—to the field of AI.

Where understanding, description, and explanation are at stake, the resolution of this stranger–nonstranger tension as follows: what is valuable is not the perspective of the stranger but the perspective of the *estranged.* The valuable and necessary thing is first to understand and *then* become estranged in order to gain the social analyst's perspective on what you have become socialized into.

Estrangement is taught in first-year sociology and philosophy courses if they are good ones. The best way to learn estrangement is in regard to your own society—learning to see your own society as strange. If the perspective of the stranger were as important as some claim it to be, then there would be no sociology of our own societies, because none of us are strangers in regard to our own societies—we have to *learn* to become strangers to our own societies. Since there is a sociology of our own societies, estrangement must be possible without one's ever being a stranger.

How do you learn to estrange yourself from your own society? I suppose you could take drugs—though I've never done it. It helps to belong to a marginal group in your own society—Jews, homosexuals, and so on—from whence you begin with a tangential view of what others take to be normal. I have always found the philosophical *problem of induction* a great help: if I can get it into my head that the state of the immediate future is not guaranteed by the state of the immediate past, so that the computer on which I am typing might suddenly melt like a Salvador Dalí watch, I can experience the present as fragile and therefore strange. The sociology of knowledge works the same way: when you realize that your deepest beliefs, even those things you would die for, are just contingencies of where you were born and brought up, then their grip on your mind is loosened to a dizzying extent. What is all this estrangement for? It is to help you see what you are experiencing, because only when you see it do you have any chance of describing it. Describing it is still very difficult, but we'll come back to that problem later.

I illustrated the possibilities of self-conscious estrangement, of course, when I explained the problem of describing spoon-bending children. Pinch and I viewed them from the perspective of a stranger coming from a place in which paranormal metal-bending was normal and physical metal bending was rare or unknown to the extent that it would never occur to anyone to believe they had seen it; this was all imagination. Now we get to some estrangement tricks.

Breaching Experiments

A classic estrangement device is the *breaching experiment*, invented by Harold Garfinkel. Garfinkel did things like ask his students to go home and act as though they were guests in their parents' house—act with exaggerated politeness and so forth. This made the parents angry because the unspoken taken-for-granted rules were being broken. I sometimes amuse myself at the cash register in supermarkets by taking goods from the section of the belt that belongs to others in front of or behind me, pointing out that "after all it's not yours—you haven't paid for it." I smile a lot and put the items back pretty quickly. My favorite is still the breaching experiment invented by Peter Halfpenny and described in the introductory chapter—getting on a bus and asking the driver to sell you two tickets, one to reserve the seat next to you.

The trouble with the breaching experiment is that before you can invent one you have to understand the society pretty well; you must already have attained the estranged perspective to see what would make for a revealing breaching experiment. It takes a lot of bringing the taken-for-granted into your consciousness to realize that in our kind of society you cannot reserve the bus seat next to you; that brilliant breaching experiment requires that the brilliance be there first. So breaching experiments, while great fun, aren't quite as good as they seem at creating estrangement from scratch; they are good ways of revealing what someone else has must already have brought to the surface.

The Proxy Stranger

A trick that gets over both the limitations of the breaching experiment and the difficulty of alternating between one way of looking at the world and another is the *proxy stranger* method. This has never been used, as far as I know, except by me and my acquaintances and students, though it is a staple of comedy. The idea of the proxy stranger is that you do not pretend to be a stranger yourself—a useless idea until you have gained a good bit of understanding—but rather ask someone who is a stranger to go into the society you know well while you look on. The person who is going into the society is acting as a proxy for your ability to invent breaching experiments—they are a proxy stranger. Watching the proxy stranger's *faux pas* brings to the surface what is taken for granted in the society in which they are immersed even if, at the outset, you know it only tacitly and have not yet brought it to conscious via your own estrangement. What you see as the proxy stranger fumbles about is a series of automatic breaching experiments that no one has had to design.

We tried some proxy stranger observations, but they were focused on low levels of the fractal and were more a matter of understanding the difference between the social acquisition of expertise and learning from instructions than doing anything more grand in the way of understanding societies. Hartland tried getting those with no medical training to take blood pressure measurements by following printed instructions.[2] Kusch and I observed a social worker who knew nothing about physics trying to follow instructions to make a vacuum pump work—he confused the vacuum pump for a pump used to deliver cooling water, which actually flowed from the tap with no intervening pump.[3] These examples of the proxy stranger method all involve science of one kind or another but, having been so little used, the method must be wide open for further development and investigation in various social science situations. To run such an experiment you are going to need a volunteer who doesn't mind being embarrassed. Being hardly ever used to date, the method is wide open for the application of ingenuity.

The Controversy Study

Fracturing the medium of social life—disturbing its smooth flow—renders its planes and plates visible: the breaching experiment and the proxy stranger method are ways of fracturing the flow. Another is the controversy study, though here the fracture is managed by the members of society, not the analyst. In the controversy study, one looks at sets of actors in dispute with one another. These are easy to find in science, but they should be discoverable in other areas of social life too. My research on gravitational waves and parapsychology began as controversy studies though, as explained, I didn't quite realize that this is what they were until later. When scientists argue with each other, one can see what they hold precious and what they are prepared to give up, and this tells you a great deal about a society. Joe Weber, as his position became precarious, was willing to give up more and more: he gave up the idea that the source of gravitational waves was the center of the galaxy and decided that it must be more local; he gave up the idea that the emission of gravitational waves was steady and continuous and decided he had been lucky enough to see a fortuitous burst; he gave up his own initial theory of the sensitivity of his detectors and developed one based on quantum theory that made them a thousand million times more sensitive; he gave up certain standard data analysis procedures and invented one that seemed to violate the second law of thermodynamics; he even flirted, at one time, with the possibility of psychokinetic effects. I learned the useful term *cherished beliefs* from the astrophysicist Kip Thorne—these are the beliefs that are the last you would give up as you try to defend a difficult position.[4] There must be an enormously strong parallel here with the sociology of religion and its conflicts with science: how much is given up, and how is it given up, as the theory of evolution erodes the literary account of creation in the Bible? One could fruitfully analyze the clash between creationism and evolution as a controversy study.

Imitation Games

Imitation Games are another way of fracturing the smooth flow of the fluid of society so as to make its plates and planes more visible. Imitation Games are related to the proxy stranger method in that they too get someone—the Pretender—to try to pass themselves off as a member of a collectivity to which they do not belong. In this book, two kinds of process—the acquisition and possession of expertise and socialization into forms of life—are treated as the same thing. Reflecting this, in Imitation Games we talk of the *target expertise*. The target expertise is the ubiquitous expertise of the domain being explored. Pretenders aim to pass themselves off as possessing the target expertise, while a Judge/Interrogator, who does possess the target expertise (i.e., does belong to the form of life under examination), asks questions intended to unmask them. Simultaneously, the Judge asks questions of a Non-Pretender who also possesses the target expertise: the Judge's job, when acting as Interrogator, is to ask questions that are good enough to reveal, reliably, who is who. Figure 7.1 represents the game.

The imitation game was the forerunner of the Turing Test.[5] In that forerunner, men pretended to be women or vice versa; in the Turing Test, the pretender was a computer. In the Imitation Game as my colleagues and I have developed it, the questions are usually asked and answered via computers linked by a local area network or the Internet, but a simple email exchange moderated by a "postman" also works well if numbers are small. Note that we capitalize "Imitation Game" and the roles within it when we are referring to the research tool we have developed rather than the original parlor game.[6]

The technicalities of the Imitation Game (IG) have been written up at length elsewhere, so here we will concentrate on discussing the features that are relevant to this book.[7] As already mentioned, the IG is another way of disturbing the smooth face of society so as to reveal its underlying characteristics. This happens because the Interrogator is forced to think about good questions for trapping the Pretender and is therefore forced to estrange him- or herself: they must reflect upon and articulate the nature of the society being explored, and these questions, all of which are recorded, can be examined by the experimenters. The Judge must then work out whether the Pretender's answers represent those of a stranger or someone who has estranged themselves from the Judge's society. The Non-Pretender also has to reflect and estrange themselves, while the Pretender's failed answers are equivalent to the responses of a proxy-stranger. That, anyway, is the idea, and the IG was first successfully used to explore the notion of

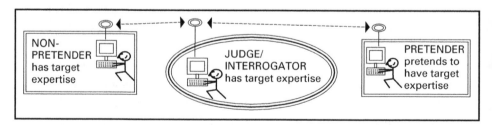

Figure 7.1
A schematic of the Imitation Game.

interactional expertise. We have used the game on a wide range of scales: individually to investigate my expertise in gravitational wave physics; in small groups to investigate the interactional expertise of the blind, or doctors with regard to chronic illnesses, and so forth; and on a large scale to investigate understanding of gays by straights, Scots by English, and the like, all at a national level.

Using the Imitation Game to Test Participatory Understanding

My answer to Stoltzenberg's question (see chapter 5), about how you know when you have succeeded in understanding a scientific group that you are investigating, was in terms of the changing nature of the interactions between the investigator and respondents—more and more interchange with regard to scientific questions (or whatever would be the equivalent in some other domain). That is quite a robust indicator, as the contrast with amorphous semiconductors makes clear. But the Imitation Game is another way of testing how well you understand the field, and the great advantage of this method is the outcome can be publicly inspected and affirmed; it's more than just the investigator's report backed up by one or two respondents. So that is why, in 2005–2006, I subjected myself to an IG test of my understanding of gravitational wave (GW) physics. The result was reported in *Nature* and even independently tested by a *Nature* journalist who had the outcome judged by an additional GW physicist of his choice.[8] I say "so that is why," but, as usual, it wasn't a carefully worked out plan, just a matter of following up a research instinct: "This would be an interesting thing to do"; "Having invented the IG method, what excuse do I have for not applying it to myself?"; "What on earth would happen if I did try this on myself?"

The episode involved my recruiting a professor from the GW group in Cardiff's physics department to ask some technical questions about the subject and pose them to me and to a genuine GW physicist from his department. It turned out that he decided to ask seven questions in one go rather than iterating question and answer, but that worked well. The session was conducted over email with my colleague, Robert Evans, acting as postman so that the origin of turns was concealed. Actually, the experiment turned out to be more complicated than this and has a number of interesting features, but that is the topic for the comprehensive

Imitation Game book that is in preparation and the outline is all that is needed here.[9] The dialogue, consisting of seven questions and seven pairs of answers, was sent to nine other GW physicists who were asked, "Who is the real (anonymous) GW physicist and who is Harry Collins?"—all of them knowing me well. Seven said they could not tell and two said I was the real physicist. We spent some time trying to work out why I had done better than 50/50—the best expected outcome—and this will be reported in the big book on IGs. As mentioned, when *Nature* learned of the experiment they sent the dialogue to another GW physicist who also said they could not tell, and they wrote a story about the event. So my understanding of GW physics was now publicly tested and affirmed! This experiment was repeated in 2015–2016 in a more informative way with a broadly similar result.[10] The more recent experiment showed how narrow—crevasse-like—specialist expertise is: even astrophysicists who shared a coffee bar with their GW physicist colleagues were little better at answering the questions than social scientists, while I did almost as well as the genuine GW physicists.

The question is whether the Imitation Game should be used by everyone involved in participatory research that involves understanding. It seems like a good idea but, without a great deal of ingenuity, it won't work outside of fairly literate groups. A university is an ideal place to conduct such a test, whether dealing with the sciences or nonsciences; other settings will require more real-time ingenuity. Furthermore, passing such a test is a very high hurdle. I would not have expected to pass that kind of test in my early years of investigation, which were based on the interviews conducted in the 1970s—indeed, if I had passed it in those years there would have been something wrong with the test. Still, it is always good to understand the compromises one is making, and even failing such a test could help one understand without undermining the research. It is clear that if I had managed to conduct such tests for my understanding of the theory of amorphous semiconductors and compared it with my understanding of parapsychology and GW physics, the result would have been highly encouraging in the case of the latter two even if I did not pass. Finally, even without physically carrying out such a test, it can always be used as a thought experiment: we can imagine ourselves subject to such a test and ask ourselves how well we would do. This ought to be another good way of thinking about how well we understand an initially unfamiliar society.

Investigating without Understanding

The final feature of the Imitation Game that bears on this book is that the original intention was to use it as a way of doing participant comprehension research but without *comprehending*. It was meant to be the equivalent of the "philosopher's stone" in alchemy—turning the lead of purely external, "objective" observation without subjectivity into the gold of research based on the actor's way of being in the world rather than the analyst's. How is this possible? It is possible because in the IG you organize actors to be proxy researchers for you: it is the actor-Judge/Interrogators who ask the questions requiring understanding, and it is the actor-Non-Pretenders who supply answers against which the answers of the nonnative-Pretenders can be judged. You, the analyst, need know nothing of the world of the actors; you need only read off the numbers to see how well or poorly the Pretenders can pass as Non-Pretenders. Each run is the equivalent of the test to which I exposed myself, and, as you can see, you need not know anything about GW physics to make sense of the results: only the GW physicists have to know about GW physics.

Well—that's not quite true; the philosopher's stone does not work as well as we had hoped. We found that even when we carried out the large-scale experiments, where we wanted no more than the numbers that represented the average pass rate of hundreds of Pretenders, we could not make sense of these numbers without making sense of the societies—for example, should religious belief in Rotterdam be such an outlier, or was there some systematic error? We found that we needed researchers who knew the societies to filter the questions and answers, because some respondents did not understand the game even after it had been explained by local assistants who did know the society. Thus, this supposedly purely statistical experiment would yield only thin outcomes, when it would yield outcomes at all, unless the meanings of the questions and answers were understood so that we could see not just the outcomes but how they were arrived at.[11] Indeed, in the early medium-scale experiments we only trusted the outcomes because we could see how they had been arrived at. But this is the subject of chapter 9, which looks more closely at the relationship between qualitative and quantitative research.

8 Bringing the Story Back Home

Hints and Guidelines Extracted from Chapter 8

• Results expressed at a high enough level can be conveyed without needing the audience to understand the society in question.

• Cross-cultural communication is much harder than people think.

• One way of conveying understanding is to use quotations from respondents.

• Quotations are exhibits, not data.

• Beware of transcription techniques or styles of analysis that take you away from the talk itself.

• Transcribe fully until you are well advanced in your career.

• Speech and text have different meanings.

• Let respondents edit their quotes.

• Consider doing some light editing on quotes yourself.

• So long as one is honest about it, consider inventing what a respondent "might have said," as novelists do, to illustrate one's understanding; but check with respondents.

Writing Up

Let's suppose we've found our way of understanding an unfamiliar society. Now we have to write up what we have found and bring it back to the rest of the sociological community as a publication. But the rest of the community hasn't been immersed in the alien society and, given that the only way to understand it is through immersion and socialization, how are they going to understand what you are telling them? This is the third of Stoltzenberg's questions, and it is just one facet of a huge discussion in sociology and philosophy about cross-cultural communication. Can we ever understand the Azande poison oracle, in which a chicken is poisoned to divine whether someone is a witch and the result is given by whether the chicken lives or dies, but a second chicken is also poisoned and its fate has to be opposite of that of the first if the verdict counts as being confirmed?[1] The answer given here is that deep enough socialization will result in this making perfect sense—as much sense as Mrs. Keech having saved the world through the cult's vigil.

There is also a question about the ability of certain beliefs to coexist in a society. Pinch and I found that it is socially impossible to use the tools of professional physics to investigate paranormal spoon-bending without ridicule: scientific society insists that one identifies oneself with one side or the other, and as soon as one makes the slightest move to take parapsychology seriously, then nothing else one says will be taken seriously by mainstream science.[2] But in what I am arguing here, we are less concerned with the social strain than with the conceptual strain that comes with interdisciplinarity, or the melding of different disciplines or activities within science—the latter problem often being discussed in the literature under the heading of "trading zones."[3] It is what gave rise to Gabriel Stoltzenberg's third query— the problem of communicating your findings when you "return home": How, if forms of life are characterized by their own frameworks of mutually untranslatable meanings, can they talk to each other?

Note that this is not the same problem as how they are learned; we know how one can acquire the meanings pertaining to forms of life, namely, by socialization. This is the problem of intercommunication in those cases where there is no translatability or socialization. And lack of translatability may be there but not noticed. Indeed, it is because it is so easy to miss that the problem of communication is so hard: both parties to the exchange believe they understand what the other person is saying, but they don't, and they don't discover that they don't until they have wasted a lot of time and given themselves a lot of grief. The example of Kusch and me struggling in front of the whiteboard over the meaning of "action" is a microscopic version of this point. The term *interdisciplinarity* is thrown around a lot in today's grant-funding agencies with, apparently, no understanding of the problems: if there were understanding, interdisciplinary grants would be funded far more lavishly—well enough for the researchers to hang around in the coffee bar with each other for at least a year before they got started, just talking about their work.

So how does a participatory sociologist who has come to understand an alien and incommensurable society explain it to the home society of sociologists who do not understand it? First let us look at some less ambitious but nevertheless important solutions. Consider the results of the 2005–2006 Imitation Game experiment with gravitational wave (GW) physicists where I was chosen as the genuine GW physicist. The result can be understood without understanding any GW physics at all—one can see, without oneself understanding any GW physics, that I did have a good grasp of GW physics in 2006 (and later in 2015), and one and can see that in 2015 the understanding of GW physics by non-GW physicists and certain sociologists was not much different, showing that specialist expertise is deep and narrow. So one way of bringing results home is to express them at high level of generality. So long as claims are trusted, audiences can be told what has been found in general terms, and these results will be meaningful. Indeed, one might say that these results are an instance of the successful application of a sociological philosopher's stone. But what if we want to describe findings in more detail? That means sharing the alien understanding.

Use of Quotations

A pragmatic approach to this problem—it is not a "solution," that is far too grand a term—is to use lots of quotations from the speech of members of the alien society. How this works I do not know—it ought not to—but it does seem a useful way of conveying what happens elsewhere. It is essentially a technique borrowed from the novelist—novelists try to convey their readers to imagined places, and the use of quotations is an attempt to do the same thing with no more logical justification than can be brought to bear on novelists' imagined worlds. But it tells you what you are doing when you record and transcribe the talk from which you are learning— you are collecting "exhibits"—spoken artifacts—to present to the folks back home.

Above all, these spoken artifacts are not data but exhibits or illustrations, showing what you have learned while you were immersed somewhere else. This is why I am suspicious of methods of transcription that involve coding that can lead to numerical analysis of speech and which take the analyst away from the speech. What you need to be doing is continually listening so as to capture the most beautiful illustrations of what you want to convey: respondents nearly always invent better ways of saying things revealingly than you can—you must sieve the gold from the rest. Knowing what counts as a good illustration or convincing exhibit requires interpretative skill—it cannot be done by counting or classifying words or utterances. When, in 1972, a physicist (now a Nobel Laureate), said to me, "That experiment is a bunch of shit," he uttered a phrase that offered a whole new world of understanding of physics to a wide audience; I could not have made it up and I certainly cannot think of any way I could have coded for the power of its transforming potential.

Transcription

That said, as already remarked, over a lifetime of research my transcription practice has changed markedly; here we'll tie some of this to changes in technology. When I began my research, a tape-recorder was a bulky instrument and the recording quality was poor—good conditions were needed if a clear recording was to be made, clear enough for easy transcription. Transcribing, of course, in those early days, was a matter of endless toggling of the playback switch and frequent use of the reverse switch to listen over and over to unclear or ambiguous passages. Later, specialist transcribing machines came on the market with foot-pedal controls and "fly-back" that would automatically rewind the tape for a second or so whenever you lifted your foot from the play pedal. Recorders became smaller, which made their introduction to new respondents a little easier; and then recording quality improved enormously with the introduction of the minidisc, making life easier again. Finally, the solid-state, digital recorder came along with its wonderful recording quality—I could now record the proceedings of an entire busy meeting without any special equipment, such as microphones distributed around the room, and listen to the recorded meeting as clearly or even more clearly than when it was live. These days, digital recorders are tiny machines that disturb no one by their presence, and the fact that the recording can be transferred to a laptop in digital form and transcribed using all manner of replay aids makes the handling of recordings almost pleasant. It might be that the age of automated transcription of recordings made in these kinds of noisy environments is on the horizon, though, since one often has to separate one voice from another; it may still be a matter of making sense of what is being said before it can be transcribed.

That is an account of the changing technology of transcription, but my practices have changed in another way. When I began my research, I transcribed everything in full, and I strongly recommend any novice researcher to do the same. But transcription takes time, however comparatively easy it is these days, and as years have passed I transcribe less and less but, rather, concentrate on dredging for gold in real time. This has been made immeasurably easier by the digital recorder, which allows you to make an index mark on the recording by pressing a button, an index mark that will show up on the transcribing device display on the laptop. This means you can mark gold nuggets in real time and retrieve them at leisure. Let me emphasize, once more, that learning to spot gold is a skill that develops along with learning to understand the society you are researching. There are no shortcuts for the novice researcher: transcribe everything, because that's the only way you are going to develop your understanding. It should be years before you relax and stop transcribing everything.

The Meaning of Speech and Text

A caveat on the use of recorded speech: you have to make sure a transcribed passage means to the reader what the speaker intended it to mean. The trouble is that transcribed speech can mean something very different from spoken speech. Once more, this finding emerges from fieldwork.

Sometime around the year 2000, I sent an extract from an interview transcript back to a respondent in the GW field study asking if he was happy for me to use it—all this was in line with my "Code of Practice for Interviews" since I intended to quote him by name. He replied that he would prefer it if I removed all the "uhms" and "ers," which gave a misleading impression of hesitancy and uncertainty. My initial reaction was to say no—I had transcribed literally, and this is what he had said. I said that if I removed the hesitancies it would look too polished, and interview transcripts were typically full of this stuff; if I removed them my colleagues would know this wasn't the real thing.

But then I thought a bit more about it: What was the "real thing"? I had returned the extract to the respondent asking him if it was an accurate representation of what he had intended to say, and he had replied that it was not. So why should I say he could not change it? The crucial point was that when he had spoken to me, though his talk was full of "uhms" and "ers," in speech these came across as place-holders while he thought carefully about what he was expressing, and gave the impression, if anything, that what he was saying was not uncertain but the outcome of very careful consideration—so *more* certain rather than less. But as the respondent had spotted, on the page, the same hesitancies gave the impression of something different. Insofar as I was using this kind of extract to convey the form of life of physics, I would be doing a bad job if what wound up on the page was different from what I had heard—it would be a badly chosen exhibit, and the golden nugget would have turned to lead. So I conceded and took out the hesitancies. My practice since that time is to allow respondents to do light edits on their transcripts if they want: what I want on the page is not necessarily some set of symbols that correspond as precisely as possible to the phonemes uttered, but symbols that would appear to typical readers to correspond to what the respondent intended to convey. To have the best chance of the written transcript conveying what the respondent meant to say, the respondent should be able to adjust the written version. This is not infallible because of the spectrum of readers' interpretative tendencies, but it is difficult to think of a better way of getting it as right as possible. Given the rationale, nowadays I occasionally do some light editing myself, taking my interactional expertise as a warrant to act as a proxy for the respondent. This is particularly relevant where nonnative English speakers are involved, because they are not in a good position to check their transcribed speech for its impact on native English speakers. If you transcribe the infelicities of nonnative English speakers too literally into English, they can come across as a bit dim, which would fail to convey the form of life in a catastrophic way. So for this kind of research, phonetic accuracy must not become a shibboleth.

There is, of course, no such thing as a "literal transcription"; the same words or sounds, when represented on the page by letters of an alphabet, can mean very different things to different people. A tragic case in England, is the 1953 judicial execution by hanging of Derek Bentley. His conviction was quashed in 1998 on the grounds that he did not do any shooting, but this was too late for Bentley. Bentley's criminal accomplice was Christopher Craig, who shot a policeman dead on a rooftop; Craig was too young to be executed. Immediately before the shooting Bentley had said to Craig, "Let him have it." This was interpreted by judge and jury as an order to Craig to shoot, and thus was Bentley considered to be the instrument of the policeman's death. But the phrase could also be interpreted as "Hand the gun over to the policeman." One would have had to hear the utterance in context to know which was intended by Bentley, but the judge and jury had only the written transcript.

Around 2015–2016 my colleagues and I did some experiments to test the difference between spoken and written meanings. We used the same interview from 2000 with hesitancies mentioned above (with the permission of the respondent).[4] We prepared two short extracts from the audio recording that contained many hesitancies and we prepared written transcripts with the hesitancies included. Using a careful experimental design, which presented the transcripts and the audio extracts in different orders to different respondents, we asked the respondents (mostly university staff and students) to score them in terms of degree of certainty expressed. The difference was so striking as to render statistical analysis otiose; the extracts were *heard* as conveying a fair degree of certainty but read as conveying much more uncertainty.[5]

Word Embedding

There are, of course, many other ways of using and thinking about recorded speech, some of which treat the construction of the speech itself as the object of inquiry and some of which treat the content of utterances as data. One impressive way to use talk, written or spoken, is in the analysis of word embedding. By building huge corpuses of words as they are uttered in a society or social group, one can harvest a certain amount of understanding of the meaning of a word from its relationship to all the other words in the corpus. This idea is in tension with my claim that meaning can be gathered only through socialization; it is the kind of tension we find at the frontiers of the argument about artificial intelligence.[6] But I had anticipated some of this in my gravitational wave fieldwork, noting that

later, conferences would happen without the physical presence of Joe Weber or even his virtual presence in the vibrations of the airwaves that constitute words. In my first day at the [1996] Pisa [GW] conference, during which I listened to every paper, Weber's name was mentioned just once, in passing. (Collins, 2004a, 451–452)

What I am trying to grasp here is the mystery of how spoken language conveys so much understanding of the world without making it explicit. I am indicating that some of it might happen in the very arrangement of words and silences. That Weber's name was not mentioned in the course of the day was telling everyone that Weber was no longer important in the science of the field without anyone saying it. Maybe patterns of word embedding in semantic nets, extracted from huge corpuses of speech, can tell us something without being a replacement for meaning.[7]

Here, then, is some melding at the edges of the immersive way of understanding and the data that can be gathered by quantitative analysis—something that has already been discussed in the context of the Imitation Game. We'll come back to the relationship between quantity and quality in the next chapters. Note that it is important not to become so convinced by a qualitative approach that one cannot even countenance a quantitative approach—one should never allow a tribal-type loyalty to a method to close the mind. We'll look at the problem again in the next chapter.

Making a Historical Record

Something else that interviews do in the case of some momentous scientific discovery like that of gravitational waves is record the words of the scientists at the important historical moment. Wouldn't it be interesting to have the words of Einstein on tape in the decades prior to his momentous discoveries, or those of Eddington when he set out to try to confirm the general theory of relativity by observing the eclipse, or Michelson and Morley—what did they consider they were up to with their interferometry experiments? It is obvious that these considerations in the case of science apply equally to other momentous political and social events. That is why it is a good thing to be honest about any editing or inventing if you allow yourself to do it—otherwise the words become useless as a historical record. As intimated above, here the primary aim is not history, but it does happen as a spin-off, nevertheless, and one should do everything one does as well as possible.

Science and Art in the Use of Interviews

To return to the extraction of meaning from immersion in a culture, it is not surprising that there is an art to using interview transcripts to convey forms of life—it is, as mentioned, a technique borrowed from writers of novels. I think my initial resistance to allowing respondents to edit their transcripts post hoc was born out of some residual feeling that I should be faithfully representing what happened in my interviews. But we are dealing with meaning, not data! The obvious question is whether it is legitimate to make up quotations to convey meanings as novelists do. I can't see why not—it follows from the logic of the argument. The important thing is to explain that this is what one is doing. Why not say, "Respondent X could have said ..., and this would have conveyed the essence of the thing still more clearly." I think it would have to be checked with respondent X, however. There is nothing unscientific about this, as what we are talking about here is not data but conveying an understanding that, in principle, anyone else in the same position could have acquired and that, in any case, you are checking with native members. Now we switch to a closer look at quantitative methods and their relationship to qualitative investigations.

9 Tangible versus Inferential Experiments and Probes versus Surveys

Hints and Guidelines Extracted from Chapter 9

• Science is not the same as technique, for example, statistical technique.
• Polarization of methods is damaging.
• Science is a form of life identified by certain "formative intentions," norms, and values.
• 2-sigma claims are barely better than chance, so there is a replication crisis.
• But 2-sigma results can be strong if the mechanism is tangible.
• Sometimes quantitative results are merely illustrative, not foundational.
• Purely statistical results are weak.
• Scientific instincts and styles evolve, even in physics.
• If the world being investigated is *uniform*, a *probe* is good enough and a survey is not required (another application of RRoMM).
• See how domain discrimination can be expressed.
• We need to understand what a group is if we are to understand when we can use probes as opposed to surveys and for what topics.

Academic Tribes

Social scientists love to assign themselves to methodological tribes. At the beginning of a career, when everything is in flux and you don't know where you are going, you can discover that you have an academic identity by proclaiming that you are a "positivist," or an "interpretivist," or an "ethnomethodologist," or a firm adherent of one of the multiple other perspectives that are available. As a member of one of these tribes, you might well learn a set of complicated and slightly mysterious words for describing straightforward things. I certainly did this when I was younger. I started off as a Popperian but when, in 1967, I discovered Winch, I become an interpretivist. The discovery served me well, guiding my thinking when I was in doubt.

The trouble with these identities is that they carry with them sets of prohibitions as well as positive hints, and the prohibitions can be damaging. This is because some of the dichotomies are believed to map onto other monolithic views, whereas life, as always, is more complicated. Thus, the broad positivist–interpretivist divide is often taken to map onto a still broader science–humanities divide along with a narrower quantitative–qualitative divide. This means that interpretivists often feel that they must not say their work is scientific or objective but cleave to being literary and subjective; they take it that they do not have a duty to generalize, just describe in a "sensitive" way. They also think that doing anything that involves numbers and calculations is incompatible with their monolithic interpretive–humanist identity. The positivists, of course, think that nothing that cannot be objectively measured is worth discussing, and even when they rely on their native understandings, as in the survey method, they studiously ignore the fact that they are doing so. Mainstream economists are worse in that they start by imagining how humans *must* behave and then construct a highly mathematical science on top of that (an example of "magical scientism"), which, thank heavens, more and more people are beginning to understand isn't about anything much except a certain kind of brilliance as assessed strictly within the economics clan. All this is terrible because it shuts down the imagination and shuts off interesting dialogue between the methods and approaches, which are far less distinct and monolithic than an inevitably polarizing tribal approach makes them appear.

Another truly costly result of the way the polarization leads to caricature is that when governments try to justify policies, they give far too much weight to quantitative analysis at the cost of qualitative. But good can come from evil: it may be that the "replication crisis" that, as should have become evident over the last few decades, besets the social sciences along with other sciences whose warrant is a relatively low level of statistical significance—nearly all of them except physics—will lead to a reassessment of the supreme value of quantitative studies. Quantity and quality have to work together if we want to understand the social and economic world.

That we, here, are in the business of eroding such monoliths should have been evident from the beginning of the book. We began by criticizing Stephen Cotgrove's *Science of Society*, which took it that surveys and statistics were what made a social science scientific. Cotgrove was reflecting what was widely believed at the time: I remember one of the UK's leading social scientists answering a student questionnaire about the essential abilities of a sociologist by saying that no one could call themselves a professional in the field unless they could do a certain complicated statistical calculation, a confusion between science and technique that was widespread at the time. The rise of the computer is fast putting an end to this nonsense since computers can generally do every kind of mathematical manipulation better than any of us, making it obvious that the science must be somewhere else. I have tried in this book to erode the humanist monolith by arguing that subjective understandings should be replicable and lead to generalized claims that can be checked by others, while I have attacked the competing quantitative monolith by arguing that interview quotations are not data but can be used after the fashion of a novelist—even allowing that they could be invented by the analyst for illustrative purposes so long as what is going on is made clear.

Science

So what, then, is this science to which, in this book, it is said one should adhere? Science is, like everything else that happens in societies, a form of life. As a form of life, it is characterized by formative action types—the things you have to do to be a scientist. Scientists do lots of things, but not all of them are formative of the scientific form of life; cheating is one example. The formative action types are driven by methodological understandings and certain rules. I'll quote from one of my books, as the claim set out there has been welcomed by some natural scientists:

It is hard to list the special values of science, because it is an activity only vaguely defined. ... One can make progress, however, by imaginatively taking away different elements and seeing if what is left can still be called science. Thus, one can take away the ability to see the face of god and still have something recognizable as science [I have in mind the fanciful description by one of the discoverers of the cosmic microwave radiation]; one can take away the best-selling books that no-one understands and still have science [I have in mind Stephen Hawking's *A Brief History of Time*]; one can take away the religious war against religion and still have science

[I have in mind Richard Dawkins et al.]; one can take away the venture capitalists and still have science [I have in mind the biological startup companies]; and one can take away the front page stories and the superstars and still have science [I have in mind Brian Cox et al.]. These features of science as a cultural institution are merely "derivative."

On the other hand, one cannot take away integrity in the search for evidence and honesty in declaring one's results and still have science; one cannot take away a willingness to listen to anyone's scientific theories and findings irrespective of race, creed, or social eccentricity and still have science; one cannot take away the readiness to expose one's findings to criticism and debate and still have science; one cannot take away the idea that the best theories will be able to specify the means by which they could be shown to be wrong and still have science; one cannot take away the idea that a lone voice might be right while all the rest are wrong and still have science; one cannot take away the idea that good experimentation or theorization usually demand high levels of craft skills and still have science; and one cannot take away the idea that, in virtue of their experience, some are more capable than others at both producing scientific knowledge and at criticizing it and still have science. These features of science are "essential," not derivative. (Collins, 2013, p. 156)

I would add to these *the belief* that sound findings are replicable and, more generally, one should seek ways to corroborate one's claims. Notice that there is nothing here about mathematics and statistics or any other kind of technique; you can adhere to all these intentions while exploring all manner of investigative avenues. Science isn't exactly what 1960s philosopher/physicist Paul Feyerabend said it was: he said "Anything goes," and it certainly doesn't. But a lot more does "go" than under the old social science concept/insult of positivism. Note that in spite of the extent to which science is opened up under the cultural definition, it is still different from the arts and humanities and in stark contrast to the emotional truths and alternative facts that are associated with Donald Trump's "post-truth" and the Nazis' "big lie."[1]

The Replication Crisis

For the last decade or so, many of the sciences have been undergoing a replication crisis. This was pointed out by Ioannidis in 2005, in a paper with the provocative title "Why Most Published Research Findings Are False." What is being referred to here is not physics but sciences that generally publish claims backed up by statistical confidence of 2 sigma—or less than 1 in 20 odds of being a result of chance. This is the level used by almost every science other than physics, not least the medical sciences, about which Ioannidis was writing. (2 sigma is also used by many areas of physics itself outside of high-energy and gravitational wave [GW] physics.) Since Ioannidis wrote, the impossibility of replicating many of the supposed findings in these 2-sigma sciences has become clear—this is the *replication crisis*. No one seems particularly bothered about it in sociology and other subjects where practitioners don't concern themselves much with replication.

Various causes and cures have been suggested in those sciences where replication is an issue. It has been suggested that the cause could be the increasing lack of care and professionalism brought about by competition for publications and resources: scientists are in too much of a hurry. It has been proposed that the problem could be ameliorated by focusing more on effect size than the statistical backup for small effects, by increasing the level of statistical significance demanded from the 2-sigma 0.05 level to 0.005[2] and by encouraging open data policies, allowing for easy replication, and a change in the culture of journals that would encourage the publication of direct replication studies.[3] But such changes, though they would be good—shifting to effect size is the best—wouldn't get to the heart of the matter.[4] We can understand the problem through a fruitful interaction between fieldwork on physics and sociology itself: the experience of physics shows that 2 sigma is never going to produce good science, and this should have been obvious even without Ioannidis. Physics has steadily increased its standards for what counts as a discovery from 3 sigma in the 1960s to 5 sigma today.[5] The standard of 5 sigma implies only 1 chance in 3.5 million of a result being due to chance, a significance that is beyond the dreams of the social sciences and pretty well all the other 2-sigma sciences. Physicists made this change because they found that 3-sigma results, and then 4-sigma results, were unreliable—things that they thought had been discovered turned out to be wrong. Only physics has the large number of readily repeatable experiments with high statistical significance to give rise to this kind of experience, but it counts for all of us. Just because your science cannot reach a 5-sigma level does not mean it does not need to reach a 5-sigma level, if it wants reliable results based purely on statistics. And physicists went for a 5-sigma level in the hope of swamping all the systematic errors and "trials factors" that they knew could still be affecting their experiments and statistical calculations; they knew they couldn't eliminate these problems so they tried to overwhelm them—with some, if not total, success. There are still discovery claims in physics that turn out to be wrong. Consider the BICEP2 team's 2014 claim to have discovered primordial gravitational waves. It turned out to be cosmic dust, not gravitational waves, after all.

So if the physicists cannot eliminate these problems, the social scientists cannot eliminate them either, whether they know it or not; indeed the social scientists are not even aware of some of the problems such as what physicists call the *trials factor*. What this means, very roughly, is that every time you try another statistical test on the same data you should cut the apparent statistical confidence in half. Imagine you are using the one-in-twenty criterion: if you do twenty different tests or cuts then one of them is almost certain to come out positive, and if you report only that one and throw the others away you are reporting nothing of any interest even if it looks like a fine result. An analogous process is said by critics to apply in sciences like parapsychology, where many unsuccessful experiments are carried out and consigned to the file drawer while the occasional successful one, which is bound to turn up by chance, is published. Taken on its own, the individual result looks good, but in the wider context it could be meaningless. I have argued that a statistical outcome is like a second-hand car: you don't know how good it is until you know the history of previous drivers.[6]

So far, we haven't mentioned the huge range of systematic errors that can and almost certainly do affect the 2-sigma sciences. However good the statistical outcome of my survey, if there has been bias in the selection of respondents or the posing of the questions then the result just does not mean what it says. Putting all this together, we can say that the sciences that report their results in terms of a statistical confidence in the low range are now highly suspect, at least so long as the result turns on statistical calculation only, and this alone should rebalance the way "scientific-looking" results and qualitative results are treated.

Tangible and Inferential Experiments and Observations
There is a way to make social scientific results more secure, however. This again applies across the sciences and is another place where we can learn about sociology from the social analysis of physics and, perhaps more

surprisingly, physics can learn from sociology. I introduce here a new classification of experiments and observations into two classes: *tangible* and *inferential*. Usually, statistical calculations are treated as though they stand alone, but when an outcome is tangible this can support statistical inference.[7] This difference emerged out of my colleagues and my thinking about our own early Imitation Game experiments. Why did we believe the results? It turned out, after a lot of reflection, that it wasn't the statistical calculations that convinced us. Sensitized by my GW case study, we could see that there were too many opportunities for systematic error, and we were, in any case, struggling to understand how to do the statistical calculation—we just weren't good enough statisticians to deliver the kind of "statistical punctiliousness" (another new, quasi-technical term) that the physicists knew how to deliver. Our solution was, once more, a matter of RRoMM—the retrospective reconstruction of method method. But before coming back to our own work let us move in the opposite direction—let us see how this insight, or reflective discovery, from social science illustrates what goes on in physics. And just before that, let us make the point made in a striking way using the example of medicine.

UBL and Parachutes   Imagine an illness called "Undifferentiated Broken Limb" (UBL).[8] A person suffering from UBL has a broken limb but we do not know which one. A treatment for UBL is proposed—namely a cast applied to the left leg. A randomized, blinded, control trial (RCT)—the apogee of statistical punctiliousness—is employed to test the treatment. The control group has a cast applied to the neck as a placebo. The RCT proves highly successful, with 25 percent of patients being cured of UBL while none of the control group gain any benefit. A cast on the left leg is widely introduced as a treatment for a broken limb. What this shows is that we use RCTs only when we understand or can observe little or nothing of the mechanism of the illness we are trying to cure. Where what is going on is understood or visible—tangible—there is no need for RCTs. A funnier example is a spoof article in the *British Medical Journal* complaining about the lack of randomized control trials for parachutes.[9] To repeat, we only reach for statistical punctiliousness when we don't know what is going on.

The 2015 Discovery of Gravitational Waves and the Airplane Event   Now back to what physics can learn from us. Joseph Weber's early claims to have detected gravitational waves were based on widely separated *resonant bar* detectors.[10] All that is expected to be seen by a resonant bar when hit by a gravitational wave is a burst of energy that slightly exceeds the background noise; that burst has no identifying features that indicate that it was caused by a gravitational wave rather than by a seismic disturbance or some other noise. Noise is measured and eliminated as far as possible, but in the last resort a *detection* consists of an *inference* from a coincidence between two such bursts on two or more widely separated detectors; the coincidence cannot be otherwise explained. A *detection*, then, consists of nothing more than the occurrence of something statistically unlikely; resonant-bar GW detections are purely *inferential* experiments. For a bar group to maintain a claim that they have seen a GW rests on the exercise of refined statistical punctiliousness, and the half-dozen or so claims that were made were subject to intense statistical scrutiny and eventual rejection by the majority of the scientific community, it being believed by many that trials factors—failures of statistical punctiliousness—were the source of the apparent statistical result.

The next generation of GW detectors were interferometers, and their advantage, apart from increased sensitivity, was that they could see something more detailed than a burst of energy. Interferometers are not resonant devices that integrate all the energy in the waveform into a narrow frequency; they can follow and record the evolving signal in real time. Theoreticians were able to model the emission of gravitational waves associated with the source most likely to be detected by the interferometers—the inspiral and merger of binary star systems at the end of their lives—and experimenters could look for these patterns. Analysts built a 250,000-strong template bank of models of waveforms modeling inspirals of two black holes, two neutron stars, or a combination of both, covering a range of possible masses for each scenario. The waveform of a detected signal could then be matched to the template bank with the nearest match open to further refinement through more careful comparison with the signal. That was how the first detection of a cosmic gravitational wave was made on September 14, 2015, the refined model being an inspiraling binary black-hole system with masses of 36 and 29 of our suns. Was this a tangible or an inferential observation?

Being embedded in the GW community, I followed the entire process of discovery in real time from the first hours to the press conferences five months later and beyond.[11] In this field, as a result of what was widely seen as a succession of false claims emerging from the resonant bar community, and because of the way these bore on the quest for funds to support the much more expensive interferometers—from hundreds of thousands of dollars for resonant bars to hundreds of millions for interferometers—a tradition of statistical punctiliousness had built up to the point of paranoia that was felt as much by the interferometer community as the resonant bar proponents. It was always going to be immensely hard, even for the interferometer community with their much more sensitive instruments, to accept that *they themselves* had seen a gravitational wave, and the difficulty had been rehearsed in two "blind injection" trials, where fake signals were secretly injected into the detectors intended to mimic a gravitational wave. The second of these was intended to mimic a discovery, but even here the community could not bring itself to call it anything more than *evidence for* a discovery.[12]

The extent to which the punctiliousness, in this case, verges on paranoia can be seen in the unfolding of the earlier airplane event.[13] GW physicists have a rule about carefully stating and then freezing their statistical protocols before looking at the bulk of their data. This makes it impossible to adjust the protocol retrospectively so as to favor one result or another, which would be a breakdown in statistical punctiliousness. But since statistical protocols need to be tuned using real data so as to be maximally effective at extracting signal from noise, the tuning is done on a small subset of data—the "playground"—before the protocol is frozen and the "box is opened" on the bulk of the data.

In 2004, this rule gave rise to a problem. It involved not a claim about a positive detection but rather a claim about whether a certain potential signal was in fact noise, but the principle is identical. The box was opened on a stretch of data after the statistical protocols had been frozen, but it was belatedly discovered that a certain significant "signal" in the data had been caused by an airplane flying low over the site of one of the detectors—it was just noise. Removing the airplane would make a significant difference to the published result. A very long and heated row ensued between those who said that the rule about freezing protocols meant that their knowledge of the cause of the airplane noise had to be ignored or they would be engaging in post hoc "statistical massage" and those who said that this would mean publishing a result that they knew to be incorrect. Eventually, after months of argument and a vote, the paper was published with the airplane event deleted. Consequently, some scientists insisted on having their names removed from the list of authors and one resigned from the entire collaboration—it was a traumatic experience for all concerned. We will come back to this event after looking at the 2015 discovery.

In spite of years of statistical caution of the kind just explained, most scientists in the collaboration were ready to start to believe that they had seen a genuine GW event within two or three days of the first appearance of the signal in September 14, 2015. The reason had nothing to do with statistical calculations. It had to do with the fact that the waveforms from the two detectors, with their 2,000-mile separation, fitted over each other fairly well, and that both signals matched similar templates in the template bank. Thus, GW physicist Peter Saulson wrote to me on September 21, seven days after the signal:

The second piece of evidence that was very important in convincing me that this was real was how well it matched very similar templates in the BBH [binary black hole] search. ... at the same moment, a small cluster of triggers in the same short-duration portion of the template space rang off at both detectors. (quoted in Collins, 2017, p. 15)

None of this meant that the physicists believed they had a discovery that could be announced to the world. They knew that such an announcement had to be supported by a 5-sigma level of confidence and that this would not be forthcoming for a considerable time and only after a lot of work. Of course, all kinds of other noise possibilities such as malicious hacking into the devices also had to be eliminated, and that is why it took five months to write and publish the discovery paper and hold the press conferences. But the important point is that the scientists became convinced of the reality of the signal because the waveform gave it *tangibility*. Furthermore, in casual discussions postpublication I found no scientists who said their belief in the result had to do with the 5-sigma result, whereas all those I spoke to said it was the matching waveforms that convinced them. Even Luis Lyons, a leading authority on statistics in high-energy physics, who had once written an article suggesting that the discovery of gravitational waves would need to be supported by a 7-sigma statistical confidence level, told me that that it was the coherence of the signals in the two detectors that was hugely convincing.[14]

What we are trying to do here is pull apart the statistical inference element in this discovery from the tangibility element. Here, for the scientists, and, as far as my casual questioning could ascertain, for the wider scientific public, it was the tangibility element that was supporting the statistical element rather than the other way around. The statistical calculation was carried out without much enthusiasm. The first calculation of the significance came out as 4.9 sigma, but more work was done, accompanied by some agonizing over whether it had an element of statistical massage:

Look, they formally established greater than 4.9—it's fucking a lot greater than 4.9, it's 5 [as you can see from the graph]. But somebody thought there would be some jerk who'd quote 4.9 and say it's not 5. So we came up with an answer that doesn't offend our standards very much, if at all, that lets us say 5.1 instead of 4.9 and we stopped some bullshit. (quoted in Collins, 2017, p. 166)

The conclusion was that there was nothing to worry about in the way of post-hocery and that the statistical calculation had been carried through with all the punctiliousness that could be mustered. So there is no comfort for the 2-sigma sciences here; what has been shown is that a large part of the scientists' confidence that that the statistics were telling a true story came from what they could see with their eyes, not from their calculations.

Of course, no one saw an inspiraling black hole with their naked eye and they did not see any waveforms; what they saw was the outcome of an immensely complex process of filtering and inference from a string of numbers representing electrical forces used to control the interferometer mirrors. The confidence that came from the overlap between the two signals and their overlap with the template was itself a matter of an implicit sense of how unlikely such an overlap would be; and that sense was eventually translated into the 5 sigma. So the tangibility is not as direct as it is in other cases. Nevertheless, the contrast with the resonant bar results is clear. Tangibility in the modern physical sciences is becoming less and less direct, as the low-hanging fruit of the science is harvested and signals have to be detected via the intermediation of more and more delicate instruments that depend on statistics. And yet, as this case shows, there is still a clear difference between one kind of experiment and another.

That the elements of the difference can be weighted in different ways can be seen by referring back to the airplane event. If the two kinds of contribution to confidence in an experimental result as set out here had been properly understood by the physicists, there would have been no need for any withdrawals from the paper's author list, or for any resignations from the collaboration. What gave rise to these exaggerated reactions was a determination to treat the statistical calculation as though it was isolated from whatever else was going on in the experimental space. The airplane was a *tangible* cause of the noise under dispute, even though it was detected by instruments, and if tangibility had been taken into account, the airplane would have been removed immediately without any grief. Here physics can, at least in principle, learn from the world of sociological research on Imitation Games, which, as will be explained shortly, is the source of the distinction between tangible and inferential discussed here.

Some change of attitude within the GW community is already evident as the contributions of the scientific cultures of physics and astronomy become rebalanced with the existence of detectable gravitational waves becoming a normal feature of our world. The recent discovery of a GW signal from an inspiraling binary neutron star system was the second most important discovery so far because it was a new source that could be correlated with its electromagnetic emissions, such as gamma rays, whereas black-hole inspirals are dark in the electromagnetic spectrum. But in one of the two detectors that saw the signal, the trace was dominated by a large glitch.[15] This was grounds for a veto of the signal according to the statistical protocols and, indeed, the signal was vetoed by the automatic detection program. So applying the very strictest standards of statistical punctiliousness would have consigned it to oblivion. But further examination of the signal indicated that it was strong and interesting, so the glitch was filtered out and the result published with no objections. As a respondent told me (September 29, 2017):

We did have formal vetoes that vetoed this event, but we've gotten used to looking into interesting things even after formal vetoes … we've gotten used to not feeling that those automatic procedures are the last word. That said, this was a "bigger lift," actually cutting problem data out of h(t)! Still, we had practice in trusting our guts over rules. I actually am surprised that not a single person (of whom I'm aware, anyway) expressed qualms in going ahead. … but the tenor of the discussion all along was that it "smelled" correct from the start, and we heard nothing to dissuade us. Just as you summarize, we could look at the Q scan ([a graphical representation of the signal which is in this case] the best representation of the [tangible] character of this measurement) and assure ourselves that we scientists could understand this event better than any automatic procedure that we'd previously invented.

Again, the contrast with airplane event is clear, and so is the contrast between formal statistical procedures and the way they are moderated by considerations of tangibility.

Imitation Games as an Example of Tangibility Justifying Weak Statistics In Imitation Game experiments conducted in the 2000s, my colleagues and I compared color-blind persons pretending to be color perceivers and vice versa, persons with perfect pitch pretending not to possess it and vice versa, and blind people pretending to be sighted and vice versa. The results were all as we expected: the color-blind Pretenders did better than the color perceiving Pretenders; those with perfect pitch did better than those without it; and the blind did better than the sighted who were pretending to be blind. We struggled to find the right way to analyze these experiments statistically. We could produce a highly statistically significant result by aggregating the results of all the experiments, justifying this by the fact that each of them supported our "interactional expertise hypothesis," but we knew a lot of what we were doing didn't meet physics' standard of statistical punctiliousness. For example, as is typical in the social sciences, we did not have enough data to work on a section of it treated as a playground before opening the box on the main body of data, as the physicists do.

The reason we believed the results were generalizable and potentially replicable was not just that every result came out in the right direction but that *examination of the dialogues* between those occupying the three roles of Judge, Pretender, and Non-Pretender showed that the experiment was working just as we expected. What the participants said to each other and the way they detected who was pretending and who was not showed us that the experiments were revealing what they were intended to reveal. Why did we bother with the statistical analysis? Because it was expected of us—just as 5 sigma was expected of the physicists—and because it supported what we were arguing. But this support was not a "proof"; it was more in the way of an illustration—as though the statistics filled the role of a diagram in a published argument, making things clearer and more persuasive. It was the post hoc search for the justification of what we had done that led to us understand the difference between the tangible and the inferential when it comes to the justification of experimental results and the role of statistical analysis within them. Of course, all this is pretty obvious once it has been said, but that fact that it needs saying is evident from the examples drawn from GW physics and from our own confusion when we initially set out to analyze our own results.[16]

Conclusion on Tangible and Inferential Experiments and Observations
The underlying problem with understanding the analysis of experimental results is that the statistical element is too often treated as something that must stand on its own, and, on its own, it determines whether the result justifies a positive claim. In fact, we already treat statistical outturns as enmeshed with other aspects of our understanding of the world in a number of ways: we do it when we take into account trials factors and the file-drawer effect, and we do it if we embrace a Bayesian approach to statistics such that our prior understanding of the world affects the statistical calculation. But we need to go further. We now know, and should have known for a long time, that results justified by anything close to the 2-sigma standard alone are not robust enough to be repeatable. This is clear from experience in physics as well as the problems that have become evident in medicine, psychology, and the like. Statistics should be treated as an independent element of experimental justification only where experiments are purely inferential—indeed, the sentence is a truism. But stating the truism allows us to see that if an experiment includes a process or mechanism that is tangible, observable, or demonstrable, statistics may play a secondary role, even a merely *illustrative* role, rather than the central role in *proving* the validity of a result. Under these circumstances, various kinds of weakness in a statistical analysis will not be fatal to the robustness of the associated scientific claim; and, in the social sciences, qualitative findings can be seen to have far more than a hypothesis-forming or illustrative role. In some circumstances, it is the statistics, once thought to be the key to science, that play the supporting and illustrative role to the qualitative findings. How different this is from Cotgrove's version of "the science of society."[17]

Uniformity, Probes, and Surveys

We can learn more about the use of statistics in sociology and the like from the natural sciences. Sociology is obsessed with representativeness, and one of the reasons that surveys and their statistical analysis look so "scientific" is that they seem to be able to calculate the representativeness of the samples they investigate. Participatory methods have no such calculations to present, and this is one thing that makes them seem to play an inferior role. In the case of the Baton Rouge bus example, however, the lived experience of a couple of individuals was enough to give rise to an immensely reliable—much more reliable than you can get from statistics—and rather large generalization. Here I explain this in more formal terms.

When you do fieldwork—or any observation or experiment—unless the circumstances are exceptional, you are, to use the philosophical terminology, looking only at *tokens* with a view to saying something about a *type*. If I look down a microscope at a drop of pond water, the drop is a token that is taken to represent the type *pond water*. Obviously, to observe, directly, the type *pond-water* you would have to look at all the pond water in the world, and that is impossible; so you look at only a token specimen of pond water. The question is then whether and how well it represents the type.

This is a question that, most of the time, doesn't get natural scientists very excited. I'll bet that when you looked at a specimen of pond water when you were at school, the school teacher did *not* introduce a discussion about how you could be sure that the drop was representative of all pond water—you just took it for granted. I am guessing that the same went for pretty well all the experiments you did at school in physics, in chemistry, and anything else; you didn't start worrying about representativeness until you got to the social sciences (unless you tried to estimate the population of insects in a field or some such).

For social scientists, the paradigm of social research—the sample survey—keeps the problem of representativeness perpetually in focus, or at least, it is an ever-present finger tilting the scales of methodological guilt. Understanding how to absolve this guilt, at least on some occasions, grew once more out of having to find a solution to the problem of our being simply unable to generate samples large enough to be statistically representative in the first stage of our large-scale Imitation Games. If stuck with stand-alone statistics (and tangibility was not going to help in the large-scale work that was looking for small effects), then all our large-scale results would have to be discarded. RRoMM was to be our savior once more.

Actually, if we had thought about it, we would have realized that the representativeness problem was there long before we began our large-scale experiments. Shouldn't we have been taking care to make sure that our samples of the color-blind and samples of those with perfect pitch would properly reflect the performance in Imitation Games of the entire populations of the color-blind and those with perfect pitch? We gave no thought to these questions because we simply did the experiment in the way that psychologists do experiments on humans. In our case, we sought volunteers from those around us at the university, drawing on members of other departments to find the persons with special qualities, and on our own department for the "ordinary" players.[18] When psychologists do an experiment on, say, reaction times among their first-year students, they don't think that the reaction time differences they are looking at will be affected by religion, income, or location of upbringing. To introduce a new term, differences in reaction times are *uniform* among first-year students. Without thinking about it, we were taking it that interactional expertise in color perception would be distributed uniformly among the worldwide population of the color blind—at least those living in broadly Western societies, because in all such societies the color blind are immersed deeply in the discourse of the color perceiving. The opposite goes for color perceivers: in such societies, they are rarely immersed in the discourse of the color blind. The point is more sharply made when we get to the "pitch blind" who generally know nothing of the discourse of those with perfect pitch. So, though we had not yet thought this through and were just proceeding on scientific instinct, we didn't care about whether our volunteers were the kind of representative samples usually sought in sociology because, quite properly, we weren't thinking of representativeness in this way. Was it the color-blind population of Cardiff University, or was it the color-blind population of the UK, or was it the color-blind population of the world that we were looking at? It didn't occur to us even to ask this kind of question. This must have been because, without thinking about it, we realized that we were dealing with a different kind of problem from that which sociologists normally think they are dealing with when they do quantitative research. Much later, when faced with a real problem of this type in the large-scale research, we found we had to think about it, and we had a nasty shock.

The ideas used to resolve the problem were worked out in 2011, first presented in public in October 2012, and published in a 2015 in a paper entitled "Probes, Surveys, and the Ontology of the Social."[19] If every member of a population is identical in terms of the question being asked of that population, then, in principle, a single member of the population will represent the entire population just as faithfully as a large sample. That is the idea of uniformity. In such a case, there is no need to survey the population to find out about it; one need only "probe" it by looking at an individual. (It is better to use a small haphazard selection of individuals to eliminate the possibility, since not all populations of living creatures are exactly identical, that the first individual you pick is especially unusual in some way.)

The naturalness of this way of thinking in lots of scientific enterprises is easily shown. Scientists have never wondered whether the Higgs bosons discovered at CERN are special Genevan Higgs bosons or represent all Higgs bosons. The same, as we have seen, goes for pond water, sodium, the language of bees, and so on. The natural sciences are replete with the assumption of uniformity, nearly always unspoken.

The social sciences also have their fair share of uniformity, also generally unnoticed, but in this case the silence is damaging. Consider something as quintessentially social as a natural language. If I want to know where the verb generally appears in an English sentence—in the middle or at the end—I do not need to conduct a survey of English speakers; all I have to do is ask one English speaker to speak a few sentences, or, if I want to be extra careful, ask a haphazardly selected few in case the one I pick is crazy, or wants to pull my leg, or is only pretending to be a native English speaker.

This assumption of uniformity is what makes much of social science possible. It is the implicit assumption behind much of ethnography and anthropology and the participant comprehension advocated here. Since even the longest sojourn in a society or social group, unless it is very small, will involve contact with only a few of its members, what is learned from those members has to stand for what could be learned from all the members—as the pond water under the microscope stands for all the pond water in the world. Here we have the same problem discussed earlier regarding the claim that an anthropologist could be a full participant in a society. Loïc Wacquant may have made himself into a boxer, but that did not make him into a cornerman. If he was to learn about being a cornerman from being a boxer, he had to learn it by being embedded in the language of boxing and acquiring interactional expertise. In any case, he learned about boxing in general from only a small subset of boxers.

The common language is what makes it possible for contact with a subset of respondents to generate an understanding of a society. Obviously, in societies or groups where the division of roles is less entrenched it will be easier. Also, the extent to which society-wide practices can be learned from a small subset of respondents will depend on the question being asked: for a modern society, at one end of the spectrum is the place of the verb in the sentence; at the other end is voting behavior and how that will affect the next election. The latter is only open to survey methods, whereas the former needs only the most superficial probe, and questions in between will reveal the social life of more or less extended societies. We assume that pretty well anyone would be able to inform you about bus-ticket buying more or less anywhere in all Western societies; we might be wrong, but it is the way to bet.

The idea of uniformity also justifies the notion of the native informant. As years have gone by, Peter Saulson has more and more become my native informant regarding the community of GW physicists; I know that when I ask him how the community is feeling about this or that, his answers will truly represent the community. As a respondent said to me on September 29 this year in respect of the binary neutron star discovery:

... We've gotten used to looking into interesting things even after formal vetoes. ... We've gotten used to not feeling that those automatic procedures are the last word. ... We had practice in trusting our guts over rules. ... The tenor of the discussion all along was that it "smelled" correct from the start there was no problem in accepting that what was said represented the collective view of 1,000 people even though there may have been some who disagreed but decided not to speak up.

Would a social survey of everyone involved in the collaboration have done a better job? In fact, it would have done a worse job, because only a few people would have responded and it would be unclear how far to trust them because their locations within the community could be wildly different, with some being novices, some being relatively isolated, and some being eccentric. On the other hand, if one knows the community reasonably well, one learns which individuals have been deeply embedded in it in a typical way for a long time (the large majority) and one learns certain people's eccentricities and how to discount some of what they say. But, to return to a theme discussed in chapter 3, this is the hardest part of coming to understand a community, and it is the part that I found eroded most quickly as the field grew while at the same time my engagement with it grew less intense from the mid-2000s onward. I found that, knowing what I knew, I could easily track down little bits of technical advances that had passed me by and rectify problems with a brief chat; but there was no easy way to come to understand the people in the field in the same way. Luckily, I knew which people to ask when it was necessary to know this kind of thing and, having been so deeply embedded at one time, a kind of second-hand knowledge came into play. Thus, consider these exchanges with a trusted respondent, set out in 2017 on page 322 of *Gravity's Kiss*. I remark to a trusted respondent:

I found the argument that [A is B because P is Q] very weird

to which he replied

A very weird argument indeed from XXXX, although perhaps not so weird considering it was from XXXX ;-)

Another time I was told:

I think before we're done we are going to have to understand whether there is any credibility to that ... and I think that's going to be a struggle because YYYY is a really smart guy and he's pretty self-confident and he will say he believes it and people have enough respect for him that they will not blow him off so I don't know how we're going to resolve that.

Differences in meaning associated with differential credibility of respondents get lost in questionnaire research and become instead a source of noise. The importance of this source of noise increases as the number of nonrespondents increases. Only some kind of compulsory supervised survey—and that is never going to happen—would have done better at rooting out the few who disagreed about the neutron-star glitch, if there were any. But in fact, because my respondent was able to say "I actually am surprised that not a single person (of whom I'm aware, anyway) expressed qualms in going ahead," we know there were no strong feelings of the kind that were vocally expressed, and that already gives us the grounds to see how the community was changing as compared to the time of the airplane event. So this kind of qualitative exploration is actually often better and stronger than a survey. And that is why, to pick one example out of the air, no one ever suggested that Howard Becker's study of "Becoming a marijuana user" should have used a survey and statistical analysis.[20]

To repeat, I think the reason that qualitative research has often been seen as deficient, in terms of representativeness, when compared to quantitative research, is that these arguments have not been understood, and neither has the way the notion of uniformity pervades the sciences. The rebalancing effect of the replication crisis and the contrast between tangible and inferential experiments and observations also serve to strengthen the qualitative approach.

But none of this is intended to reintroduce antiquantitative tribalism: understanding-based research can sometimes be strengthened and made more beautiful with quantitative reinforcement and illustrations, and finding ways to support and illustrate quantitatively is a fascinating exercise in ingenuity. And, of course, lots of social science inquiries can only be done quantitatively—cases where there is no uniformity such as inquiries into voting intentions, average income, class distribution, and so on. The problem with sociology, to make the point in a different way, is that it tends to take nonuniformity as the default position and qualitative research is thrown onto the defensive, whereas an even balance would be better for the discipline and much, much better when it comes to policymaking. The way to start methodological analysis in the social sciences should be with an inquiry about how the notion of uniformity relates to the topic under investigation.[21]

Notice that uniformity has a relativistic component. All native English speakers exhibit uniformity in where they place the verb, but they are nonuniform in their dialects and use of "restricted and elaborated codes." But *within* a dialect they are, again, uniform, and, of course, uniform classes of elaborated code users could be found, and likewise for restricted code users. One can always find a uniform group so long as one asks a sufficiently general question. Are humans uniform in their religious beliefs? No. Are members of the Seventh Day Adventist Church uniform in their religious beliefs? Yes. Therefore, while it is correct to talk of uniformity as something that either exists or doesn't, it is also necessary to bear in mind that one must look for the right thing in the right place.

To repeat a point I made in the opening chapter, if we did not have some sense of the uniformity and extension of the social groups we inhabit we would hardly dare go beyond our front doors. That is why we can have some confidence that we can recognize situations of uniformity and justify a probe approach in ways that have a chance of being widely accepted. There will be cases where the justification is disputed and these, again, may overlap with ordinary life. For example, there is an ongoing argument about whether, and in what if any respect, lesbian, gay, bisexual, and transgender people constitute a single group with a shared LBGT identity as opposed to a set of groups, each with its own distinct and different identity. My argument is that the degree of uniformity will vary according to the question being asked: the probe logic could apply to the LGBT group so long as what one was trying to understand was the general experience of belonging to a sexual minority, but it would be a mistake to assume that the experiences of lesbian women were necessarily the same as those of gay, bisexual, or transgender people. Choosing to work at this more general level may lead one to ask if the uniform features might extend to a yet higher level and include other minority groups who also experience discrimination, such as religious or ethnic groups. All this is what you would expect to be asking under the fractal model (see chapter 1): different substantive uniformities are found at different levels.

What we need is a theory or taxonomy of uniformity to help with this kind of inquiry. It seems likely that a group will be uniform in respect of more rather than fewer research questions when, in network terms, it is fully, or nearly fully, connected, as in the densely connected black nodes of figure 9.1. Examples of such groups include local cultural minorities with strong shared identities, such as those based around sexuality, religion, ethnicity, music, or sport, such as we were investigating in some of our Imitation Game experiments. In figure 9.1, the left-hand diagram shows such an ideal scenario, though we might normally expect a few links to be missing, as in the central parts of the other two illustrations in figure 9.1.

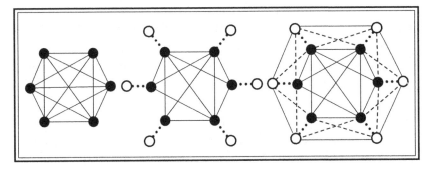

Figure 9.1
A densely connected network with some outsiders.

The reason the theory gets complicated is that there can be uniformity where the population is not maximally connected. An example is latent social groups, such as people suffering from medical conditions such as irritable bowel syndrome or dental anxiety that require regular appointments with a medical specialist but who do not belong to any patient support group. In the middle diagram in figure 9.1, the white nodes represent patients who interact regularly with one of six specialists who, by virtue of their shared training and workplace, form a densely networked group. Here the patients are isolated from each other, and so any shared understanding of their disease will be created through their interactions with the uniform medical culture. The doctors may also come to understand what it means to have the disease as a result of their conversations with the patients, but this experiential knowledge can only reach other patients if it is relayed by the doctors. In other words, to the extent that there is a joint understanding of the illness, it is the doctors who facilitate the sharing of culture, not uniformly dense sociometric connections among all the parties.[22]

The question that the theory of social groups will need to answer is how like each other these white patient-nodes will be: the doctors will be a uniform group, but will the patients be a uniform group? It is tempting to say no or, at least, that they will be less uniform, because they are not densely interlinked, but this may be too hasty. Consider natural-language-speaking communities and the case of verb placement. The links between nearly all the members of a native-language-speaking community will be indirect, with young children, for example, being only sparsely linked into the community except through their parents. Prenursery children will learn to speak language uniformly with all other prenursery children (e.g., in terms of verb placement) while linked into native-language-speaking society only through their families. So there must be a way of getting strong uniformity at the top level of fractals with only sparse sociometric ties.

The right-hand diagram in figure 9.1 shows patients each interacting with several specialists and also with each other through the formation of a patients' support group (probably with denser relations between patients than is shown here). Two questions arise in this scenario: first, would the patients become more similar to each other than is the case in the middle diagram; and second, would there be any tendency for the patient group and the doctor group to draw apart and develop their own distinctive practice languages?[23] Working these things out seems to be one direction sociology ought to be taking if it is not doing so already.

Then again, the uniformity of social groups is not fixed. Nowadays we see red-headed people trying to form a solidaristic group, but it seems unlikely that they have been successful as yet.[24] Our theory would have to explain when and in what respects such a collection of people does become a sociologically recognized collectivity and whether it is uniform. The boundaries and qualities of "groupishness" within social collectivities thus becomes a topic in its own right—incidentally, a topic to which the Imitation Game can be applied, as it can be used to measure social solidarity.[25]

10 Against Tribalism: Alternation and More

Hints and Guidelines Extracted from Chapter 10

• There are different levels of alternation and different kinds of social courage; the fractal model is key.

• Things change during a very long-term study, such as emotional commitment and political ambience.

• The emotional loyalty required to establish a new way of looking at the world may need to be relaxed to build a useful discipline.

• Therefore, avoid cultish tribalism while not giving up what is of methodological or substantive value—and never fall into sloppiness.

• Different levels of the fractal involve different kinds of conceptual relationship with respondents—with higher levels giving rise to shared problems.

• RRoMM is an imperative when the approach changes; it drives innovation and keeps everything straight for the reader.

Alternation and Social Tension

Alternation comes in a variety of flavors and requires very different types and levels of courage. Now we have switched from talking of conceptual strain to social strain. To alternate between gravitational wave physics and ordinary society requires at the very least a technical courage—how is one going to work with the most brilliant scientists in the world in a not-too-deferential way and acquire enough of their technical understanding to make it work? It also requires the courage to know when one has failed, as I did in the study of amorphous semiconductors. But the study of gravitational wave physics also demands a different kind of courage: I had to continue to take Joe Weber's long-discredited findings much more seriously than the scientists as time went on if I was to maintain my methodological relativism. The scientists' world was reconstituted in part by coming to treat Weber as a maverick, whereas I had to continue to treat him seriously. This kind of courage was more like that required to research parapsychology symmetrically; to do that, one has to make oneself an outcast from most academic society, including sociological society. (In the late 1970s, I had a rather good paper on parapsychology rejected by the *American Journal of Sociology*, who said they would welcome a similar paper if I wanted to write one about a more mainstream subject. It was very disappointing to discover that my chosen discipline was so conservative and judicious. The ideas eventually would turn up in chapter 2 of my *Changing Order*.) Keeping track of Mrs. Keech's millennial cult's view of things would have involved even more self-conscious estrangement from day-to-day reality and, should we have announced ourselves as even just temporary "Keechists," we would probably have been exiled from academic life.

But in all the cases described in this book, given that they are all set in Western society, any contradiction between social and/or conceptual worldviews is being explored in the context of an overarching sharing of worldviews. Indeed, the differences are explored through conversation in a common natural language in which pretty well everything else is mutually understood. The research on conceptual ruptures rests, then, on my respondents and me sharing our ubiquitous expertise: the regular means of communication, transaction, and travel, the norms of dress, cleanliness, manners, and so on. One has to reach for the fractal model to understand how these things work, and how some things change while others stay the same.

Investigating scientific controversies means that the organization of the work is driven by the unfolding of the science, and the studies can be very long-term. In early summer 2016, I gave a talk about the discovery of gravitational waves in a university well known for its influence on the sociology of science. The press conference announcing the first detection of gravitational waves had taken place in February of the same year, and many people in the STS (science, technology, and society) field understood that I had been watching for decades and that this was a triumph, not only for the science but for my persistence. I talked about the science of the discovery and my disappointment with the way it had been presented to the public by the physicists.

In the question session, an old colleague, from the early sociology of scientific knowledge days, opined that I had lost my intellectual way. A few months later when I reopened the discussion with him, he emailed me: "I was trying to say how struck I was by the contrast between your early work and more recent stuff. ... The former was bold, radical and puzzling— part of what drew me into science studies (and structured my work for years). The latter basically mimics the scientific propaganda machine. ... It occurred to me to try suggesting to you that you'd forgotten all the aspects of science that you'd once helped us to see." This started me thinking about the many different ways in which I relate to science studies, to the field of GW physics, and to the different things one can do with a case study.

Let us start with longevity. Here I am going to say something about the history of science studies, but the issue applies to many areas of sociology and, no doubt, other disciplines as well. I've already said that proclaiming loyalty to a style of analysis can provide the novice researcher with an identity, but disciplines also have a youth and maturity. Because of the longevity of my studies, I've lived through different epochs of the history of science studies, and that accounts for quite a bit of what my colleague thought he was perceiving.

There are sociological imperatives involved in establishing something radically new—something that involves a new way of thinking. In the early days of the sociology of scientific knowledge, the fierce emotional loyalty to the constructivist way of seeing the world exemplified by my old colleague was a necessity, because we were inventing a new form of life with its own new taken-for-granted realities. Establishing such a thing is hard, and it was especially hard in the case of science because of what science was taken to have accomplished during and immediately after the Second World War. This meant we were trying to establish a radically new way of thinking about science in the face of enormously powerful forces. These forces woke from their slumbers during the "science wars." As a result, we had to do everything we could to establish and support our cognitive determination. Unwavering loyalty to the new way of thinking was essential. At that time, the emotional impact of the new kind of alternation that was being invented regarding science had the dizzying quality that Peter Berger talks of and, I believe, critics were right to fear it. If taken seriously, it does pose a threat to our society, as I have intimated throughout.[1] But nearly half a century has passed since those heady days; the "new way" of thinking is now solidly established and certainly not in need of continual proclamation, except perhaps in the undergraduate essay.

As explained in earlier chapters, it is still necessary to cleave to the analytical and methodological relativism that is the basis of sociology of scientific knowledge because it is vital if we are to do good work on the social causation of any kind of knowledge. As it is, the basic message of the need for alternation is still being missed by some of the groups who analyze science from the outside, and therefore it still needs stressing from time to time. For example, some philosophers are prone to accept scientists' results at face value and then present these as a supposedly "philosophical" critique of fringe science—showing it to be "irrational" or some such. How one approaches these things should depend on exactly the work one is trying to do. To repeat, when one is trying to explain why scientists come to believe "this" rather than "that," one should never invoke the material world because the scientists themselves cannot invoke it with certainty; and if one is trying to explain why one religion triumphed over another in some location, one should never invoke the intrinsic superiority or validity of one faith over another because that is not sociology, it is proselytization. Obviously, no sociologist of religion would invoke the spiritual world as a sociological explanation, and it remains a puzzle to me why sociologists would invoke material causes rather than sticking to what they know— social causes. Scientists don't invoke the material world when they argue among themselves in a scientific controversy, because they don't know how the material world will look pending the outcome of their work; rather, they invoke the outcome of their experiments, their cherished beliefs, and their judgments of trust—something quite different. Only when the scientists have settled their arguments is a new material entity legitimately added to scientists' and sociologists' ubiquitous expertise—but by that time, the sociological and historical work has been done.[2]

But, with that need for *methodological* astringency in the sociology of scientific knowledge recognized, do we still need the kind of fierce adherence to a narrow approach that characterizes certain sociological tendencies long after their new idea has been established? We now have things to do with all that has been learned from those early days, and doing these things means modifying the cult-like adherence to a style that can cauterize the imagination. My work on AI and on expertise emerged squarely out of what I discovered using the relativist approach, but both bodies of work use the *findings*, not the *approach*, instead adopting the natural attitude of the scientist. There is nothing fundamentally antagonistic to science in adopting a relativistic attitude to scientific knowledge, so there is no reason not to adopt a scientific attitude when applying the findings. This kind of switch between approaches should never degenerate into sloppiness—the mixing of a bit of relativism here and a bit of common sense there—a malaise to which the sociological study of science in particular seems prone, since its original relativistic stance was so hard to maintain. This is why the retrospective reconstruction of method method should always be applied when the approach changes or turns out in unexpected ways. RRoMM it is not just an amusing term for making excuses, it is an imperative: one must find a way of keeping everything straight in an explicit way, not simply adopt whatever approach is convenient. This applies whether it is a new method that is being developed or a shift in theoretical understanding. Furthermore, trying to make sense of things when one discovers a problem is a driver of innovation—the experimenter's regress and the distinction between mimeomorphic and polimorphic actions (see chapter 6, note 5) grew out of striving to create some sense when faced with a problem and an inconsistency, respectively. Above all, when mistakes have been made or the approach has varied, it is one's academic duty to describe and explain. To fail to do this is dishonest and, worst of all, leaves the reader in the terrible position of trying to make sense of inconsistent work. It can take years for a novice to have the confidence to say of an authoritative text "That does not make sense" rather than "My understanding must be faulty."

Another problem with cleaving too much to a disciplinary style is that it directs academic interest away from how the world works and toward the way the discipline works: it turns from looking outward to looking inward. To repeat, there are moments when an inward-looking obsession is important, but those moments do not last forever in either an individual's life or that of a discipline; obsession has to be transformed at some stage into, at best, a duty of methodological care. Mainstream economics seems to be an example of a discipline that has become pathologically inward-looking, placing purity and ingenuity of technique first while forging a discipline that explains the world comes second. Likewise, ethnomethodology, which produced so many insights in its early days, seems to be driven nowadays more by form than content.[3] And social studies of science is a field that is also in danger of putting philosophical ideology above innovation, given some of the interchanges I have been engaged in and anonymous referees' reports I have encountered.[4] Nearly all these novel approaches to social analysis that, out of necessity, begin by demanding cult-like loyalty have something to offer, but it must be recognized that once the heady creative days are over, unlike the way they continue to be presented and justified by some of their uncompromising advocates, they don't offer everything.

Again, we need adherence to at least methodological relativism for the sake of analytic efficacy in sociology of scientific knowledge, but we need to lift our gaze when, from time to time, other projects come into view. We need to lift our gaze if we are to use our new analytical skills and knowledge to best effect.

The long duration of the studies described here has also taken us from one political epoch to another. Unless we are going to set ourselves on some mythical academic pinnacle, sociologists of science should be ready to admit that the political ambience of the times has a bearing on how they analyze findings. Where sociology of scientific knowledge came in was with Robert Merton's famous norms of science, which it is impossible not to believe were a response to the growth of fascism in the 1930s; Merton was surely trying to get the "ought" of antifascism from the "is" of an efficacious science.[5] What we were doing was replacing his model with an approach more suited to the free-wheeling sixties, when those dangers seemed to have dissipated. And, of course, we were the first social analysts to get right inside science, and the descriptions and analyses we produced were far superior to those abstract norms and other schemas. It is unsurprising, however, that those with long memories feared what we were doing, and they were right to fear it even if the reaction of trying to suppress the new analyses, rather than try to understand them, and work out what to do in the light of them, was misplaced.

Nowadays, we find ourselves in a neo-Mertonian moment, with the attack on truth and the growth of populist movements reminiscent of the dark days that gave rise to the Second World War. Surely it is time to try to invent something compatible with the new thinking that can fill the role of Merton's arguments. This would mean that today's sociology of science, while retaining all the methodological and substantive findings of the revolutionary days of the 1970s, would turn its gaze in a different direction suitable to a new set of problems. We call this proposal the Third Wave of science studies; it gives a special place to expertise, and to science as a bulwark of democracy.[6]

Some Regular Sociology

If one is engaged in a long-term case study driven as much by the unfolding of the topic as by the home discipline, various other aspects of what is going on may give rise to interesting sociological findings. The analyst remains a person of sociological sensitivity watching social lives unfold. In my gravitational wave studies, I found myself analyzing all sorts of things that were not deeply based in sociology of scientific knowledge and the relativist imperative. These include *Pascalian funding*, which has to do with how it is that the military is far more ready to fund wild scientific projects than the civilian sector because of the different balance of cost and benefit in the two sectors; *evidential collectivism and evidential individualism*, which have to do with the extent to which scientists believe insecure findings should be released for public scrutiny before they are thoroughly investigated; and the differences between *small science and big science*, which was part of the unfolding history of gravitational wave physics and explained some of the tensions in the field. Each of these analyses could be said to arise out of the particular professional sensitivities and forms of expertise of the sociologist, if not the sociologist of knowledge, but once explained they are readily understood by scientists and may well be embraced if they are thought to be useful for scientists' work. Certainly one or two scientists sometimes talk to me nowadays using the term "evidential collectivism," and I have even been asked to lecture to a National Science Foundation meeting for scientists on the nature of big science.

Likewise, when I wrote up the discovery of gravitational waves in *Gravity's Kiss*, the book published in 2017, the main analytic hinge was how it was that the scientists came to believe that they had found something and how it came to be accepted by the wider community. To show what this acceptance comprised, I worked out ways to disbelieve it—for example, all we saw was a string of numbers and the rest was interpretation; the statistical procedures could have been questioned; and I reported on the views of the fringe of scientists who did not believe it. This was all to show that the "logic of scientific discovery" actually turned on scientists' willingness, at some point, to stop exploring every possible avenue of doubt; if they had been unwilling to do this there would have been no discovery and, indeed, no science. So this aspect of the book should have pleased my colleague who complained that I had lost my disciplinary purity.

But there was another part of the book that turned not on disciplinary imperatives but just on sociological sensitivity. I complained about the way the physicists presented their results. I said they wanted to draw this momentous discovery out of a hat, like a stage magician's rabbit. Consequently, they had to keep secrets for five months from September 2015 until the February 2016 press conference, with the result that many in the community, including me, had to lie to journalists and deceive our friends, acquaintances, and family members. I thought there was no need for this and set out my complaints and an alternative procedure in chapter 13 of the book. I was particularly incensed—remember, I was close to being a full participant—by the physicists' refusal to acknowledge, at the time of announcement in February 2016—and they did not spill the beans until June—that they had seen a second strong and convincing gravitational wave signal on December 26, 2015 (the Boxing Day event), a couple of months before the first press conference. It was this signal that dissolved much nervousness about the reality of the first detection, as physicists are never happy with reporting only one instance of a phenomenon—they have been caught out that way before. So I found myself worried about the secrecy, uncomfortable about the lying and deceit in which I was a participant, and really angry about the concealment of the Boxing Day event, which seemed to me to falsify the history of the discovery and the reasons for the community's overwhelming certainty. In this passage of the book there was no issue of incommensurability, no need for alternation or for disciplinary purity. Should I be ashamed of this? I don't see why. This was the physicists and me disagreeing (mostly—many younger scientists agreed with me), while speaking the same language of secrecy, deceit, and the nature of science.

Around the same time, my friend Peter Saulson, the gravitational wave physicist, led a seminar in our sociology department at Cardiff, in 2017, where he contributed to the discussion of tangible and inferential experiments (see chapter 9). Having this kind of dialogue between the home discipline and the subject under study is nothing to be ashamed of; on the contrary, it is enormously rewarding.

I think the best way to understand all of this, once more, is in terms of the fractal model. The deeply disciplinary stuff happens at lower levels of the fractal, whereas the more ordinary analysis that involves no alternation happens at higher levels where, technical understanding aside, a lot of understanding is shared at the outset. The question of the nature of science is found at a high level of the fractal as far as the physical sciences are concerned, and it is a topic for both me and my respondents.[7] What I was feeling was that the scientists I loved for providing a fifty-year-long object-lesson in how to do academic inquiry and how to live a life based on reason with integrity, were, at this moment of discovery, letting everyone down in the matter of the right way to present science.

To understand the heat I felt, one needs to go still higher up the fractal, to the level of the public understanding of science. The February 2016 press conferences about the discovery were the lead items in that evening's national news bulletins and, as such, they placed my case study right in the domain of ubiquitous expertise. The "rabbit out of hat" style sits with "face of God" pronouncements and the popular books that are as comprehensible as the Latin Bible and just as fervently worshipped. All these do a disservice to ubiquitous expertise and stand in the way of science being a lead institution for democracy. Science is a craft practice, and the detection of gravitational waves is one of the greatest examples ever of human perseverance in peacetime. It should be presented as an exemplary passage of craft work carried out by a community of the highest integrity and extending over fifty years of heroism in the face of scorn: it should not be presented as a highly funded version of stage magic, or a new kind of religion—that model is going to disappoint over and over.

Worse, the fractal model is something the citizen must understand, at least implicitly, if society as we know it is not going to erode. In two recent books and one under submission, my colleagues and I have used the gravitational wave physicists as a model of perfection for democracy.[8] We argue that the kind of expertise exemplified by the physicists is the kind of expertise that the citizen has to learn to trust. Citizens have to judge the weight to be given to opinions emerging from the various levels of the fractal model of society depicted in figure 1.2. One must understand where the relatively trustworthy elements of the fractal are located if we are to preserve the kind of democratic society we have and not pass all decision making to the powerful or celebrated. Citizens need the right meta-expertise! Citizens need to understand that the craft workers I had watched for nearly fifty years were the kind of people to be trusted because they, not the celebrities or the billionaires, are the most honest people in our society and, even though they cannot get everything right, they will be using every atom of their disinterested experience and perseverance to try to do so. In the 2017 book, Evans and I argue that disinterested science is the one institution whose values might survive even the erosive force of free-market capitalism. That's one reason why it is better if scientists do not take too much notice of the sociology of scientific knowledge, and when we sociologists of science do our own work we too should forget about it.[9]

We cannot avoid the charge that sociology of scientific knowledge and its successors have the potential to give comfort to post-truth politics in general.[10] It seems to me, therefore, that the time for the language of those fierce and necessary emotional attachments of the early days is past. The way the sociology of scientific knowledge is used now—and, as I have said, it is still essential to use it as a method of analysis—should be a matter of analytic and political judgment. Other perspectives, such as the Third Wave, which continue to embrace the rich findings that emerged from the emotional days, seem more needed than ever, and there seems to me no reason at all, as a case study unfolds, why sociological sensitivity should not be applied in as many ways and at as many levels of the fractal as seem interesting.[11]

11 Saving the Science of Sociology

Hints and Guidelines Extracted from Chapter 11

• Sociology is the study of the social and the consequences of socialness; that is what gives it identity as a discipline.
• The pond–field fallacy: fuzzy borders do not mean there are no distinct territories.
• What stereotyping means and does not mean.
• Groupism can be evil, but groups are the basis of sociology.
• It is persecution of people in groups, not classification of people into groups, that is evil.
• It looks like we have been building a science of sociology.

Groupism and the Meaning of Sociology

In the introductory chapter, I pointed out that what I would be doing here was sociologically unfashionable because it champions science, and might even be seen as politically reactionary, as the stress on groups could encourage stereotyping and prejudice. But it is only in certain circumstances that what Brubaker calls "groupism" is misleading and dangerous.[1] Brubaker argues that when it comes to ethnic groups, we should turn our attention from thinking of them as homogeneous explanations of aspects of behavior, such as intergroup conflict, and instead look at the ways groups become *defined* as homogeneous and how, when these definitions are taken up, they can enhance conflict. Brubaker is right, but his vivid writing and the very term "groupism" can lead readers to believe that all uses of the idea of social group are politically reactionary. Brubaker condemns "the tendency to represent the social and cultural world as a multichrome mosaic of monochrome ethnic, racial or cultural blocs," whereas, so long as the "ethnic" and "racial" are deleted, and the monochrome is carefully qualified, the phrase is a perfect description of the view that has been championed here: that "the social and cultural world *is* a multichrome mosaic of (mostly) monochrome blocs" is exactly what the fractal model advertises, albeit with some multidimensionality smearing the colors.[2] This is how sociology has to look at the world if it is to be its own science. But the "monochrome" has to be qualified over and above the multidimensionality reason: *bad* stereotyping takes it that if one knows the social origin of a person, one knows everything about that person, whereas individuals do escape from the determinism of the groups within which their persons were originally formed, often as a result of a huge effort of estrangement, sometimes as a result of encounters with unusually varied experiences, and sometimes because groups overlap in complex ways. Nevertheless, given the enormous and overwhelming determining influence of where and how you were born and brought up, the starting point has to be overlapping cultural blocs.

It is true that, in modern societies, collectivities overlap more and more and the boundaries between them can be muddy, while globalization and mass media reveal different existences to us as we grow and mature. To use the current terminology, there is *intersectionality* among groups, and for some members of some groups this is their most important and salient feature. On the other hand, if one picks the right question, generalization about groups is not only the right way but the only way to explain much of what goes on in our lives: all English speakers tend to put the verb in the middle of the sentence, and no religious Muslims eat pork. And if one goes low enough in the fractal of mutually embedded and overlapping social groups, one is also likely to enter social territories where uniformity of action and understanding is a fact, and it had better be if qualitative sociology is to have a warrant. To give one small example drawn from my big case study, in 2017 all gravitational wave physicists know the special, technical meaning of *little dogs* whereas no one else does unless they have read my books.[3]

Of course, stereotyping can be used in evil ways through inventing and ascribing undesirable tendencies to groups, or even inventing groups where no social identity exists. But to react to this by insisting that groups in general do not exist within identifiable conceptual worlds is ontologically absurd—society makes no sense under such an approach, and neither does sociology. The very notion of intersectionality draws on the idea that *there are groups to be between* and the idea of positive discrimination rests on the idea of generalizable social distinctions.

A popular kind of argument among social scientists works from fuzziness of borders to the nonexistence of classes, but it is fallacious—the *pond–field fallacy*. Thus, if there is a pond in a field it is impossible to say precisely where the pond starts and the field ends because the borderline is, in this case, literally muddy; but it remains that one can drown in a pond but not in a field, so water and earth are distinct even though the boundary between them cannot be defined. Let me add, in case the mud is taken to be a negative metaphor, that it has its special properties too: it is mud you need for a mud bath, and while you can only grow corn in field, not a pond, it is only at the boundary that you can grow rice. In social life too, boundaries are often exceptionally fertile. In spite of this, prejudice is often directed against those who inhabit borderlands, and this is evil: the group idea should never be used as a source of discrimination and constraint. But that does not mean there are no generalizations that follow from the notion of social uniformity; without such generalizations, sociology is lost. The deep problem is not the distinctions but the discrimination.

Let us try to make this still more clear by using the example of the worst case ever of the evil results of classification—the Nazi genocide. Is it possible to generalize about the actions and conceptual world of twentieth-century European Jews? Probably! If one were looking for such generalizations one might start with typical religious education, which stresses the varied interpretability of texts in the hands of scholars. One might go on to the historical prohibition of certain kinds of occupation, which leads to a tendency to choose professions that are not tied up with ownership of agricultural land. And one might look at the long history of persecution by host societies that precipitates views of the world that grow out of marginalization rather than secure membership of society. But, these narrow features aside, Jews are a hugely diverse people even to the point of being hard to define. What is more, the borderline between Jew and non-Jew is fuzzy, and the central characteristics assigned to the Jews by the Nazis were a fantasy. Does this mean that the reason the Nazis were wrong to persecute the Jews was because not all Jews are the same, there is a spectrum of Jewishness, and the Jews did not fit the central characteristics that the Nazis assigned to them? No, that is not why it was wrong for the Nazis to persecute Jews! It was wrong for the Nazis to persecute the Jews because it is wrong to persecute anyone. *That is all!* It might make it a bit harder to argue for the persecution of a group if their boundaries are unclear and one refuses to do any typification in case it supports the wrong kind of stereotyping, though lack of clear definition and a refusal to engage in group talk was never a problem for the Nazis. But the wrongness is in the persecution, not the analysis; if persecution can be avoided only by refusing to acknowledge social classification then the problem has not been resolved, merely camouflaged. Classifying into social groups and analyzing their typical characteristics is what makes sociology a distinctive science; to refuse to classify in case it might give comfort to persecutors is to take a nut to try to crack a sledgehammer. Of course, sociology should do all it can *not* to use the idea of groups to amplify divisions or to misuse them as moral or political levers. Remember, also, that it is possible that sociology, through its investigations, might well show that some of what have long been thought to be groups exhibit no social coherence or uniformity; this is one, not infrequent, outcome of methods used to explore group uniformity, such as the Imitation Game.

It Feels Like a Science

In the introductory chapter, I suggested that sociology was essentially about forms of life or collectivities, and I explained that the start of this way of thinking had begun for me with reading Peter Winch's *The Idea of a Social Science* and interpreting it as a philosophical version of the Durkheimian approach to sociology, in which the social is treated as real. It is only in retrospect that I can see how this idea has driven nearly every sociological thing I have done over the fifty years that have passed since I first read Winch's book. The main title of my first book was *Frames of Meaning* while the main title of this one is *Forms of Life*: the more things have changed, the more they have remained the same.

Starting with a strong idea like this and sticking with it seems to have worked well for me. I recommend it, though, once more, I think I have been lucky (you may not think so) to have picked an idea that carried me through. Do not take this kind of luck as a condition of research, because there aren't many big ideas. Indeed, this may be the only sociological idea that will work in this way, because it seems to be the timeless basis of sociology as a unique science: sociological fashions come and go, but the idea of the social—the idea of form of life—is what makes sociology *sociology* as opposed to social psychology, or psychology, or political agitation, or semiotics, or anything else.

Let me try to illustrate what still seems a lucky choice, even though it may be the only available choice. I have worked on quite a few different ideas, but the main ones all mesh together. Much of the time this has been happening below the level of consciousness, and I have noticed how well things fit only in retrospect. A striking instance is the Imitation Games, which we began in the early 2000s; it was only after a while that Rob Evans and I noticed that Imitation Games were all about interactional expertise, an idea that came from somewhere else entirely. I remember the sudden dawning of the realization that a technique that grew out of an interest in artificial intelligence was a test of an idea that grew out of an interest in expertise. The streams of work were quite disconnected in their origins as research projects, but now one can see that they were joined at the hip in terms of the notion of social collectivities. The critique of artificial intelligence grew out of the work on knowledge that showed knowledge could not be the simple aggregative thing that the enthusiasts for the AI-trend of the time—expert systems—said it was. And that work on knowledge began with the idea of tacit knowledge that started with forms of life and continued to a full-blown social constructive way of looking at the world. The interactional expertise idea began with our treating expertise as membership in an expert community rather than something you were good at in an absolute sense: yes, an expertise was something you were good at—that was absolute enough—but the thing you were good at could be anything, so long as the members of the domain believed it was worth being good at it: it didn't have to be anything true or have useful consequences. What you were good at could be reading tea leaves or econometric modeling of economies and it was still an expertise. And one kind of expertise was interactional expertise, so it should have been no surprise that the Imitation Game had something to say about it: it is hard now to see why this was not obvious.

To repeat, most of what my colleagues and I have done is all connected together through the form of life idea, but I did not fully realize this until I wrote this book. The interconnections have made themselves felt as

I wrote. It has been a series of pleasant surprises, summed up in the follow-ing list:

• The analysis of tacit knowledge arose directly out of form of life-thinking (Polanyi contributed only the term *tacit knowledge*).[4]
• Relativist SSK (sociology of scientific knowledge) was a full-scale expres-sion of the notion that everything is forms of life and that even science and mathematics can be described in this way (alongside the identification of Winch's treatment of the germ theory with Kuhn's paradigms, which are best seen as forms of life in science).
• For those who know the sociology of science, the experimenter's regress came from combining form-of-life thinking with the idea of tacit knowledge.
• The AI studies were applications of what the form-of-life approach had taught us about science to the problem of AI—which can be seen overall as the problem of making machines participate in forms of life in the way that humans participate in forms of life.
• The more recent successes of AI, as has been seen in this book, can be treated as a positive empirical test of form-of-life-type claims.
• The discussion of expertise, along with its overall framework called the "Third Wave of science studies,"[5] began as an attempt to escape the ter-rifying consequences of SSK's extension of the sociology of knowledge to everything (astonishingly, consequences not understood as terrifying, but lovingly embraced, among many in STS).
• The substantive treatment of types of expertise as forms of life dissolved the many paradoxes of treating them as defined by their "esotericity" and special relationship to the truth; it gave rise to useful novelties such as interactional expertise, the three-dimensional model of expertise, and the fractal model.
• The Imitation Game was, first, an attempt to explore the substance and extent of forms of life.
• The Imitation Game was, second, a new method for understanding the relationships between groups in societies.
• The political implications of the form-of-life treatment of types of exper-tise provided a way of understanding what is wrong with societies that are based around populist politics—too little respect for expertise and the wrong meta-expertise among the citizens when it comes to weighing the relative importance of the florets of the social fractal.[6]

Looking back on all the connections and relationships, it feels as though, rather than doing "this project" followed by "that project," we have been inadvertently *building a science*! One investigates this and one investigates that, but there is something underlying it all—the fundamental unit of investigation—that pulls it all together into one big enterprise. That science, to repeat, is the science of sociology, because it is the science of the social.

Afterword

Sociology ought to be an exciting and vital discipline—the queen of the sciences, as August Comte once claimed, in that the different things that are taken for granted in forms of life are the basis for every other kind of conclusion about the way the world is. In the West, the right kind of sociology seems more needed today than it has been for a very long time. The right kind of sociology would begin with the fractal model and the idea of uniformity as figures 1.1, 1.2, and 9.1. We have, all of us, to understand how society works in terms of the distribution of expertise or populism will take over, and we have to understand the mechanisms that lead solidaristic beliefs to form at different levels of the fractal. Of course, the second part of this is already partly understood by advertisers, media magnates, fascist dictators, terrorist recruiters, and analysts of social media, but we need a case-study-based theory that can give us more than the understanding we have. We need to understand and promulgate meta-expertise of the social fractal if we are to comprehend how expertise fits with democracy and how democracy can be rescued from itself and its overenthusiastic champions. We need this and also an understanding of uniformity to have a chance of knowing what to do next when we see that the president of the United States, the most powerful nation in the world, allows that it is not a bad thing for groups of civilians to march into town centers, wearing camouflage uniforms, carrying assault weapons, and displaying the icons of slavery and 1930s fascism, as a way of expressing their freedom. We need to understand democracy better so that we know what to do about it without destroying it, and we need to understand groups better to know what to do about making sure that certain of them don't lead us places we have not been for eighty years and do not want to go again.

Unfortunately, the sociology of knowledge sweeps the rug out from under every kind of reassuring argument, to dizzying effect. I have already remarked that the sociology of scientific knowledge is dangerous and needs to be balanced with an understanding of the role of expertise in society—but that, it can be said, is "just one view." Sometimes I feel that the sociologist's world is too terrifying a place to live in, and so should everyone who understands it properly. So I'll finish with a remark that goes against nearly everything said in this book. In spite of what the sociology of knowledge may teach us, we must have a basic sense of the difference between good and bad, and we must nurture it.

Appendix 1: Code of Practice for Interviews (circa 1997)

http://sites.cardiff.ac.uk/harrycollins/code-of-practice-for-interviews/
(NB: check with your university's ethics committee before using this.)

Unattributed Quotations

In general quotations are unattributed. On occasions, even when quotations are anonymous, insiders can guess the author because they know the style or the substance. Often this does not matter because insiders already know speakers' positions in the debate. If there are grounds for concern the paper is sent to the person quoted prior to publication.

Attributed Quotations

No attributed quotation is ever published without a request for permission from the speaker.

The expectation is that respondents will check each quotation for accuracy. It is not expected that respondents will withdraw permission for the use of attributed quotations en masse because they do not agree with the analysis. Use of such a veto in order to influence the analysis threatens the scientific independence of the project.

Confidentiality

Both of the above are subsumed under the general promise of "confidentiality." Confidentiality means "acting honorably when trusted with a confidence." It means never using information in such a way as to embarrass the person who has provided it. To put this into practice, anything potentially embarrassing is checked with the person being discussed, and/or the person being quoted, or a third party.

Likewise nothing is mentioned that could be potentially hurtful unless it is an integral part of the historical or sociological theme. Again, the advice of others is sought when there is doubt.

Responsibility of Respondents

If no response to a request for permission has been received within a month, it is taken that no problem has been encountered and that any permission requested has been granted. [Usually, requests are made by email. They are usually repeated and every effort is made to ensure the address is current.]

Experience So Far

The above arrangements have been followed in respect of recent publications and potential publications. Some changes have been made as a result but no serious problems have been encountered (except for one incident which led to me to include the *italicized note* above).

Appendix 2: Works by the Author Making Substantive Contributions to the Chapters

Book or paper (often with a more detailed version of the argument)	Chapters
Collins, H. (1998). Socialness and the undersocialized conception of society. *Science, Technology and Human Values, 23* (4), 494–516.	1, 8, 11
Collins, H. (2004). *Gravity's shadow: The search for gravitational waves*. Chicago: University of Chicago Press.	1, 5, 8, 9, A1
Collins, H. (2017). *Gravity's kiss: The detection of gravitational waves*. Cambridge, MA: MIT Press.	1, 3, 9, 10
Collins, H. (2011). Language and practice. *Social Studies of Science, 41* (2), 271–300.	1, 6, 8
Collins, H. (1982). Special relativism: The natural attitude. *Social Studies of Science, 12*, 139–143.	1, 6, 10
Collins, H., Ed. (1981). Stages in the Empirical Programme of relativism: Introduction to *Social Studies of Science, 11* (1), Special Issue: "Knowledge and Controversy: Studies in Modern Natural Science."	1, 3, 7
Collins, H. (1985). *Changing order: Replication and induction in scientific practice*. London: Sage. (2nd edition 1992, Chicago: University of Chicago Press.)	1, 3, 7
Collins H., and Evans, R. (2007). *Rethinking expertise*. Chicago: University of Chicago Press.	1, 3
Collins H., and Evans, R. (2016). Probes, surveys and the ontology of the social. *Journal of Mixed Methods Research, 11* (3), 328–341.	1, 9
Collins, H. (2018). *Artifictional intelligence: Against humanity's surrender to computers*. Cambridge: Polity Press.	1, 6, 8
Collins, H. (2016). Reproducibility of experiments: The experimenter's regress, the statistical uncertainty principle and the replication imperative. In Harald Atmanspacher & Sabine Maasen (Eds.), *Reproducibility: Principles, problems and practices* (pp. 65–81). Hoboken, NJ: Wiley.	1, 9

Book or paper (often with a more detailed version of the argument)	Chapters
Collins, H. (1984). Concepts and methods of participatory fieldwork. In C Bell & H. Roberts (Eds.), *Social researching* (pp. 54–69). Henley-on-Thames: Routledge.	2
Collins, H., & Weinel, M. (2011). Transmuted expertise: How technical non-experts can assess experts and expertise. *Argumentation, 25* (3), Special Issue: "Rethinking Arguments from Experts," 401–413.	3
Collins, H. (2009). Walking the talk: Doing gravity's shadow. In Antony Puddephatt, William Shaffir, & Steven W. Kleinknecht (Eds.), *Ethnographies revisited: Conceptual reflections from the field* (pp. 289–304). London: Routledge.	3
Collins, H. (2004). Interactional expertise as a third kind of knowledge. *Phenomenology and the Cognitive Sciences, 3* (2), 125–143.	4, 5
Collins, H., & Evans, R. (2015a). Expertise revisited I—Interactional expertise. *Studies in History and Philosophy of Science, 54,* 113–123. (A preprint is available at https://arxiv.org/abs/1611.04423.)	4, 5
Collins, H. (2004). How do you know you've alternated? *Social Studies of Science, 34*(1), 103–106.	5
Collins, H. (1983). The meaning of lies: Accounts of action and participatory research. In G. N. Gilbert & P. Abel (Eds.), *Accounts and action* (pp. 69–78). London: Gower.	5
Collins, H., & Kusch, M. (1998). *The shape of actions: What humans and machines can do.* Cambridge, MA: MIT Press. Collins, H. (1990). *Artificial experts: Social knowledge and intelligent machines.* Cambridge, MA: MIT Press. Collins, H., & Pinch, T. J. (1982). *Frames of meaning: The social construction of extraordinary science.* Henley-on-Thames: Routledge and Kegan Paul.	6
Collins, H. (Forthcoming). The concept of alternation and the sociology of scientific knowledge. In M. Pfadenhauer & H. Knoblauch, *Social constructivism as paradigm: The legacy of the social construction of reality.* Henley-on-Thames: Routledge.	6, 10
Collins, H., & Evans, R. (2017). *Why democracies need science.* Cambridge: Polity Press.	6, 10, 11
Collins, H., & Evans, R. (2014). Quantifying the tacit: The imitation game and social fluency. *Sociology, 48*(1), 3–19.	7, 9
Collins, H., Evans, R., Weinel, M., Lyttleton-Smith, J., Bartlett, A., & Hall, M. (2017). The Imitation Game and the nature of mixed methods. *Journal of Mixed Methods Research, 11*(4), 510–527.	7

Book or paper (often with a more detailed version of the argument)	Chapters
Collins, H., Hall, M., Evans, R., Weinel, M., & O'Mahoney, H. (Manuscript in preparation). Imitation Games: A new method of investigating societies. Cambridge, MA: MIT Press.	7
Collins, H., & Pinch, T. J. (1981). Rationality and paradigm allegiance in extraordinary science. In H. P. Duerr (Ed.), *The scientist and the irrational* (pp. 284–306). Frankfurt: Syndikat [in German].	8
Collins, H., Evans, R., & Gorman, M. (2007). Trading zones and interactional expertise. In H. Collins (Ed.), *Studies in History and Philosophy of Science*, *38*(4), Special Issue: "Case Studies of Expertise and Experience," 657–666.	8
Collins, H., Evans, R., & Gorman, M. (2017). Trading zones revisited. https://arxiv.org/abs/1712.06327.	8
Collins, H., Leonard-Clarke, W., & O'Mahoney, H. (2016). Uhm, er: How meaning varies between speech and its typed transcript. https://arxiv.org/abs/1609.01207.	8
Collins, H. (2013). *Gravity's ghost and big dog: Scientific discovery and social analysis in the twenty-first century.* (Chapter 17.) Chicago: University of Chicago Press.	9
Collins, H. (2011). *Gravity's ghost: Scientific discovery in the twenty-first century.* Chicago: University of Chicago Press.	9
Collins, H., & Pinch, T. (2005). *Dr. Golem: How to think about medicine.* Chicago: University of Chicago Press.	9
Collins, H. (2014). *Are we all scientific experts now?* Cambridge: Polity Press.	10
Collins, H., Evans, R., Durant, D., and Weinel, M. (Manuscript under submission). Populism, science and democracy.	10

Bonus Extra: When Interviews Don't Go According to Plan— A Quiz

As we have seen, not all fieldwork goes according to plan, and often this results in a much more interesting outcome to the research so long as one is light on one's feet. Sometimes, however, as the following description shows, plans go wrong with less fortuitous outcomes. This brief quiz will indicate if you have understood the lessons of this book (with special thanks and apologies to my gracious interviewee).

Answer all questions in your own time and discuss your answers with an experienced sociologist.

Scenario 1

On July 22, 1996, a sweltering day, Professor "X," an experienced sociologist of science, was to conduct an interview in a laboratory near "Busytown," Italy. The night before the interview Professor X awoke with a burning sensation in his stomach. In the morning he found himself to be suffering from a typical traveler's indisposition.

Questions
(a) Should Professor X have telephoned his interviewee and called off the interview?
(b) Should Professor X have eaten breakfast anyway because it was already included in the bill and consisted of three cups of café-latte, yogurt, fruit juice, and croissants?

Scenario 2

Feeling increasingly distressed, Professor X drove into Busytown in a small and noisy car without air-conditioning. He took several wrong turns. Following the map provided by his hosts, and with luck and perseverance, Professor X located the physics department where he believed he was due to conduct his next interview. He was five minutes early. The attendants at the door told him that the people he had come to see worked somewhere else.

Questions
(a) Should Professor X have realized that the map he had been sent, while it showed the physics department, also showed arrows directing him from the physics department to the satellite location some fifteen miles outside Busytown and that, therefore, he need not have entered Busytown at all?
(b) Should Professor X have written a learned paper on the deep ambiguity of maps and their essential cultural relativity?

Scenario 3

Feeling steadily more uncomfortable, Professor X drove to the satellite location and met professor "Youngman" in the otherwise deserted laboratory. Professor Youngman and Professor X began to talk about the technical details of the apparatus that Professor X had come to see. They did this by referring to some diagrams and photographs hanging on the wall of a narrow corridor. Five minutes into the session Professor X explained to Professor Youngman that he could no longer support himself; leaning backward against the wall, he slid slowly down into a sitting position. Entering into the spirit of things, Professor Youngman also slid to the floor so that he and Professor X, still talking, sat side by side against the corridor wall with their legs stretched out in front of them.

Questions
(a) Is it ever permissible to sit on the floor while carrying out an interview in a professional setting?
(b) Is it a good or a bad thing if the interviewee adopts a similar unconventional position?

Scenario 4

A further ten minutes into the discussion, Professor X, realizing that he was about to topple into a fully recumbent position, averred to Professor Youngman that he—Professor X—was losing his grip on himself as a human being.

Questions

(a) Should Professor X have lain down immediately hoping that Professor Youngman would once more follow his example and lie down himself while continuing to talk as though nothing unusual was happening?

(b) Should Professor X have explained to Professor Youngman that his body was about to dissociate itself into random cells floating in liquid pools?

(c) Should Professor X have changed his profession?

Scenario 5

Professor X struggled to his feet and asked Professor Youngman to show him to the washroom. He explained that he would be gone for some time.

Questions

(a) Is extended use of the washroom in a Western scientific laboratory compatible with good fieldwork practice?

(b) Is it better or worse if the laboratory is small and with resonant acoustics?

Scenario 6

Emerging, Professor X requested of Professor Youngman that he be shown somewhere where he could "sit down for a few minutes." Professor Youngman took Professor X to a couch in his office. Professor X lay down on the couch and slept for about an hour, snoring loudly.

Questions

(a) Is it ever good practice to take a nap during the course of an interview with a respondent?

(b) If you answered "yes," is an hour too long or about right?

(c) What is the role of snoring in the sociological fieldwork interview?

Scenario 7

Waking up, Professor X averred to Professor Youngman that he must now leave and that he looked forward to many fruitful meetings in the future. Professor Youngman did not try to detain him and Professor X departed promptly.

Questions

(a) Should Professor X have tried to continue with the interview at the risk of further embarrassment?

(b) Should Professor X have sworn a solemn oath to Professor Youngman that he would never again return to Italy?

(c) Should Professor X have demanded that Professor Youngman swear an oath of *omerta* or silence in respect of the incidents he had witnessed on pain of "vendetta"?

Scenario 8

Professor X drove for a further five hours to get to Airporttown. Driving in unbearable heat he found it vital to relax at each service area in turn, not every one of which was spotlessly clean.

Questions

(a) Was this an example of a typical day's fieldwork?

(b) Was this an example of a bad day's fieldwork?

(c) Was this an example of the way social scientists misuse taxpayers' money?

(d) Was this an example of the futility of a relativistic approach to the sociology of knowledge in that the involuntary character of certain of Professor X's actions thoroughly refutes social constructivism and indisputably demonstrates the existence of a real world exterior to, and independent of, cultural forces?

Acknowledgments

I thank two anonymous readers for giving fulsome approval to the book proposal. I gained enormously through the generous reading of the first draft by Charlie Thorpe and Willow-Leonard Clarke; both read very quickly and made comments that led to substantial changes and considerable reorganization. Three anonymous referees then read the first submission with great care, making many assiduous comments that caused me to alter many features of the book. One of these referees sent back a heavily annotated draft manuscript from which I learned a great deal and which caused me to remove various sections and add a few others, including what wound up as the bulleted lists at the head of each chapter. My editor at MIT Press, Katie Helke, has been supportive throughout, also making sharp judgments about what should be in and what should be out. Those who don't appreciate the Bonus Extra should lay the blame at her door, along with that of Jim Collier, who reminded me of its existence long after I had forgotten it. I also thank Judy Feldmann for assiduous and sympathetic copyediting. Otherwise, all faults and infelicities are my responsibility.

Notes

Chapter 1

1. *The Science of Society* (London: George Allen & Unwin, 1968) was for many years the standard (high school) sociology text in the UK.

2. Ioannidis (2005).

3. The first detection was reported at a news conference with worldwide coverage in February 2016, but the signal had impacted the LIGO detectors five months earlier, in September 2015.

4. My bus-riding example was inspired by a "breaching experiment" invented by Peter Halfpenny.

5. This second gravitational wave was not announced until months later in June 2016.

6. This is known, as we will see, as the *fractal model*.

7. Charles Thorpe suggests a similar position is expressed in Marx's *Theses on Feuerbach*: "Feuerbach resolves the religious essence into the human essence. But the human essence is no abstraction inherent in each single individual. In its reality it is the ensemble of the social relations." https://www.marxists.org/archive/marx/works/1845/theses/theses.htm.

8. I think this might resolve the enigma of "the self." We ask ourselves how there can be a self when all the cells of the body are replaced at relatively short time intervals and, of course, our personalities change throughout our lives. But we can locate a particular set of collectivities that is associated with our material body, large elements of which never change even if there are a few additions and deletions over time.

9. The idea of formative action types is worked out in Collins and Kusch (1998).

10. Including "taken-for-granted reality" (Schutz, 1964); "paradigm" (Kuhn, 1962); culture (Kluckhohn, 1962; Geertz, 1973); subculture (Yinger, 1982); "microculture" and "idioculture" (Fine, 1979, 2007). As the opening sentences indicate, in this book

I make no attempt to find all the places that ideas not dissimilar to those mentioned here might have been mentioned in the existing literature. I think of all these approaches as just variations on one big idea.

11. Wittgenstein scholars sometimes interpret "form of life" in a biological way, taking their cue from his "If a lion could speak we would not understand him," but I take the more sociological meaning from Winch (1958). Winch's book was actually written as a critique of sociology: he claimed that the investigation of social actions was really philosophy, since actions were just the other side of concepts. But the claim can equally be read backward, or even-handedly—the important thing is understanding that actions and concepts are two sides of the same coin.

12. Collins and Evans (2007). The table is part of an approach known as Studies of Expertise and Experience (SEE), which turns on expertise being seen as a matter of socialization into expert groups; tacit knowledge is explored and analyzed in Collins (2010).

13. At one of our expertise conferences we tried playing dwile flonking to see if we could determine if it was a genuine form of life. A number of people got wet and drunk but I do not remember if the problem was fully resolved—perhaps more research is needed!

14. As sociologists know, all science is based on trust—otherwise each individual scientist would have to reinvent the whole of science for him- or herself without relying on results produced by others. So the whole of science is based on immersion in the same swimming pool and, indeed, based on the same scientific method that led Gary and me to our conclusions about Baton Rouge buses.

15. See also Collins (1998).

16. Most radically deconstructive analyses of the nature of culture can be ameliorated by using the analogy of the growth and persistence of natural languages. Actually, "analogy" is too weak a word, since language is such a central part of culture.

17. To look at it from the Wittgensteinian "form of life" point of view under which the meaning of words is their use in society, without a society words would have no meaning. I say "aspects" of our knowledge because much of it is tacit and cannot be stored except within live talk and actions and cannot be transmitted except via some form of socialization. For biological research that bears illuminatingly on this animal-human difference, see, for example, Dean et al. (2012). Note that there is nothing here that says that apes, dolphins, birds, and octopuses might not have vestiges of human-like language, but to treat them as more than vestiges is to fall into a deep pit of misunderstanding. It is the richness of our language that makes us human.

18. To anticipate the possibility of certain misunderstandings, there is a big difference between language and information exchange. This difference is explained in

detail in Collins (2010) and (2018)—the latter asking the question of what fully intelligent machines would need in terms of language.

19. To follow up on this kind of argument, see Collins (1998), "Socialness and the Undersocialized Conception of Society," or any of my books on artificial intelligence: Collins (1990) or Collins and Kusch (1998). For an accessible work directed at the latest developments in AI, see Collins (2018), *Artifictional Intelligence*. The latter uses sociological reasoning of the sort advertised here to argue against our enchantment with the intelligence of computers.

20. And there remain good reasons for being careful with subjectivity. Nothing in this book is an excuse for sloppiness.

21. For discussion of this paradox, see Collins (2016b).

22. See Pinch (1981, 1986).

23. The idea of presenting findings with maximal "evidential significance" seems to neglect the problems mentioned earlier of how to present findings to an audience that has not undergone the same socialization process as the investigator. But that problem of *justifying* findings where there is no common socialization remains even where there is high evidential significance.

24. For an excellent analysis of why numbers are trusted, sometimes more than they should be, see Porter (1996).

25. See Collins (2017). To be fair, it should be said that the waveforms were extracted using quantitative methods even if the rightness of their form and their coherence was a matter of "subjective" judgment (see, e.g., Collins, 2017, p. 15).

26. For the difference between experiments and demonstrations ("displays of virtuosity"), see Collins (1988).

27. For my take on the science wars, see http://sites.cardiff.ac.uk/harrycollins/the-science-wars/. See also Labinger and Collins (2001).

Chapter 2

1. Festinger et al. (1956).

2. The book is Collins and Pinch (1982).

3. Since we are our own notebook, it might be asked how this method compares with *autoethnography*, the method involving introspection about the analyst's own life. It seems accepted that there are two kinds of autoethnograpy (see Anderson, 2006). In *evocative autoethnography* a single actor describes their experience—a form of storytelling that actively eschews any kind of general analysis for reasons that come under the general heading of postmodernism. Why this is classed as sociology

or ethnography is hard to see as it is so individually based. It is also antipathetic to description with high levels of evidential significance and there is no reason to think it should be replicable or scientific so it has almost nothing to do with the method described here. *Analytic autoethnography*, in contrast, is ready to generalize from experience and does have a lot in common with the method described here. The difference is that in analytic autoethnography the analyst takes whatever their existing social situation has to offer for reflection and analysis whereas the participant comprehender has to enter an initially strange social group and painfully acquire new understanding; the participant comprehender will try this for a number of different social groups. Also, the autoethnographer of whatever type draws on the experience of one person only, whereas the participant comprehender draws on an entire social group; but, where there is strong uniformity, this does not make much difference (chapter 9).

4. Webb et al. (2000); the museum example is theirs.

Chapter 3

1. I was doing this work in the 1970s when times were very different: the only pressure was to do interesting work, not finish your PhD. In fact, I didn't even bother to finish my PhD and was not granted it until 1981 (by submission of publications by a member of the university faculty—fourteen papers and a book), and by that time I was a well-known, internationally recognized academic. So while I think it is much better to have a guiding idea rather than a plan, as in my experience plans nearly always fail (and when they don't fail, they result in less interesting work than when they do fail), this is a rather self-indulgent claim for someone writing in 2018. You may have to work out a plan and try to stick to it for the sake of you and your supervisor. So please forgive me to sticking to my experience; my generation was a lucky one.

2. Weber was the first person to claim to have detected gravitational waves and became famous, or notorious, for his claims. He first set out his ideas in the late 1950s, but the high point of his claims were the late '60s and early '70s. By 1975, his claims had largely lost credibility. I initially interviewed him twice, in 1972 and 1975, the first account of the work being published by me in 1975 while I published a much more complete account in 2004—listed in the reference list as Collins (2004a).

3. Fine (e.g., 2007) thinks this and, in sociology of science, Latour and Woolgar (1979) set out the position clearly. We'll come back to this debate.

4. Incidentally, in 2017, the speaker, Rai Weiss, would win a Nobel Prize for the detection of gravitational waves.

5. See Collins and Weinel (2011); the paper that marks the beginning of the third wave is Collins and Evans (2002), with the fully developed "Periodic Table of

Expertises" being published in Collins and Evans (2007). Collins and Weinel (2011) modifies the Periodic Table.

6. For a polemic against any kind of coding of textual material, see Biernacki (2012).

Chapter 4

1. In Collins (2007), I analyze the role of mathematics in physics and show that it is not as central as has sometimes been claimed.

2. Collins and Sanders (2007).

3. Contrast this with the claim made by Alan Sokal I quoted in chapter 1. Sokal does not understand interactional expertise and how much his life as a scientist depends upon it.

4. Though it took me a while to realize the connection between the two streams of thinking and the term *interactional expertise* was not invented until later, the idea can be found in my earlier work on artificial intelligence where it is relevant to the question of whether computers can be intelligent if they do not have the kind of human-like body that enables them to engage in human-like practices. The crucial counterargument is that congenitally disabled persons have normal human bodies but are able to be linguistically fluent, so the full range of human practices cannot be essential to what we can now describe as "the acquisition of interactional expertise."

5. The concept of interactional expertise has many other applications and areas of significance, which have been assembled in Collins and Evans (2015).

6. Collins and Harrison (1975).

Chapter 5

1. Methodological relativism is first explained in Collins (1981a).

2. The table in figure 5.1 is taken from Collins (2018), *Artifictional Intelligence.*

3. See Kuhn (1962).

4. Actually, Pinch complained on reading this passage in 2017, that I did not embrace the Californian world as deeply as he did. I was not interested in the hippie lifestyle of the physicists we encountered, who not only believed in parapsychology but wanted to embrace a whole way of chilled-out, consciousness-changing, Eastern-religion-related living. He wanted to settle into hippiehood while I found it tedious and was interested only in the conflict of worldviews that could be found in the laboratory; I thought these presented a much sharper tension for the analyst. But to Pinch I had not swum deeply enough. For another account of the hippie physicists, see Kaiser (2011).

Chapter 6

1. This is sometimes known as the *double hermeneutic.*

2. Winch (1958) refers to what is built on top as "technical categories."

3. See Collins (2008).

4. Those who have tried to hold on to two such views at the same time—such as Malcolm Ashmore (1989)—have wound up tying themselves into unproductive, if amusing, reflexive knots.

5. This is from Collins (1998), a paper called "Socialness and the Undersocialized Conception of Society" that was strongly influenced by my having to explain sociology on my website. The idea of mimeomorphic and polimorphic actions is found in Collins and Kusch (1998). A mimeomorphic action is one such as saluting, or synchronized swimming, where the aim is to execute the action with the same visible behavior each time. In the case of a polimorphic action different behaviors can or must be used to execute the same action: "greeting" is an example, for a greeting executed with identical behaviors every time (unless it is a salute) soon turns into a joke or an insult. The hard thing for both artificial intelligence and an "external" science of society (one that does not turn on understanding), is to make sense of polimorphic actions because the proper execution is quintessentially sensitive to social context. See also Collins (2018).

6. My helpers were Bob Draper and the late Rodney Green.

7. The book is *Artifictional Intelligence* (Collins, 2018).

8. Collins, Green, and Draper (1985), shared the prize for technical merit at the British Computer Society conference Expert Systems 85, held at Warwick University. Collins (1990) got a mention in Margaret Boden's (2008) history of AI and, according to Google Scholar, this taken together with Collins and Kusch (1998) has been cited nearly a thousand times as of December 2017. More recent praise from software testers can be found at http://www.developsense.com/blog/2014/03/harry -collins-motive-for-distinctions/.

9. Incidentally, for those in science and technology studies, actor/ant network theory (ANT) cannot give rise to an applied metasociology because there is nothing it forbids. For example, it has nothing to say about the competence of intelligent machines since there is no concept of socialness under ANT: everything is associations, not collectivities, as it bases itself in the sociology of Tarde not Durkheim. Also, ANT has no fundamental unit of explanation since everything, human and nonhuman, enters its explanatory web. Or to put this another way, insofar as it has a fundamental unit of explanation, it is words—this, of course, is unsurprising because ANT arises out of semiotics.

10. For those with some understanding of sociology of science, *symmetry* is Bloor's (1973) term.

Chapter 7

1. The book is Latour and Woolgar (1979).

2. Hartland (1996).

3. Collins and Kusch (1998).

4. Philosophers of science will recognize the relationship to the Duhem–Quine hypothesis (Duhem, 1981) and to Lakatos's (1970) idea of the difference between core and peripheral beliefs.

5. Turing (1950).

6. Development of the Imitation Game, including specialist software, was funded by a European Research Council Advanced Grant and a Proof of Concept Grant (269463 IMGAME and 297467 IMCOM).

7. For a lengthy explanation of the technicalities and practice of the Imitation Game see Collins et al. (manuscript in preparation) and Collins, Evans, Weinel, et al. (2017).

8. Giles (2006).

9. Collins et al. (manuscript in preparation).

10. I give more details in Collins (2017) and Collins (2018).

11. See Collins, Evans, Weinel, et al. (2017) for an exploration of the relationship between statistics and understanding in the large-scale Imitation Game.

Chapter 8

1. Wilson (1970).

2. Collins and Pinch (1981).

3. This term is from Galison (1997). For a more detailed analysis, see Collins, Evans, and Gorman (2007, 2017).

4. Thanks to Bill Hamilton for allowing us to use his words in this way.

5. The full experiment, the experimental design, and the scholarly background to the work is described in Collins, Leonard-Clarke, and O'Mahoney (2016).

6. See, e.g., Collins (2018), *Artifictional Intelligence*.

7. The deep-learning people hope it might tell us everything.

Chapter 9

1. For a more detailed examination of the values of science, see Collins and Evans (2017), chapter 2. For more on post-truth and the like, see Collins et al. (manuscript under submission).

2. Benjamin et al. (2018).

3. For a theory, or nontheory, of who counts as a satisfactory replicator, see chapter 2 of Collins (1985, 1992).

4. Introducing Bayesian priors has also been suggested—giving more weight to findings you believe are likely than to those you think are unlikely—but scientists can disagree about priors.

5. Franklin (2013); Collins (2017).

6. Collins (2011a, 2013, ch. 5).

7. I presented an initial argument, based on the Imitation Game research, about the relative weight of statistics and tangible findings to a 2006 physics department seminar at Pennsylvania State University, but this has not been published. A similar idea has been put forward in Clarke et al. (2014), a paper that stresses the importance of understanding the mechanism of an effect and how this understanding reinforces any statistical conclusions. The authors deal especially with evidence-based medicine.

8. This example is taken from Collins and Pinch (2005), chapter 1.

9. Smith and Pell (2003).

10. Collins (2004a).

11. See Collins (2017).

12. For the history of rivalry and the consequent growth of statistical punctiliousness, see Collins (2004a); for analysis of the blind injections, see Collins (2013).

13. See Collins (2011) or (2013), pp. 27–32.

14. The discussion is reported in Collins (2017), p. 231. Lyons's (2013) article is "Discovering the Significance of 5 Sigma," arXiv:1310.1284.

15. Abbott et al. (2017).

16. Results of the early Imitation Game experiments can be found in Collins and Evans (2014b); a complete account of the technical development of such experiments can be found in Collins et al. (manuscript in preparation).

17. The difficulty with polemical opposition to quantitative methods and quantitative methods alike is that they are unable to recognize the way each can support the

other. Biernacki (2012) finds zero good in coding, while I know of no advocates of quantitative methods who are ready to put them forward as "merely" an illustrative and interesting support for the interpretative approach; they have to be "proof."

18. Psychology departments often insist that their own undergraduates act as experimental volunteers, and one of the criticisms of experimental psychology, though it is usually made in a jokey way, is that psychology's topic is the psychology of psychology undergraduates.

19. The public presentation was at the meeting of the Society for Social Studies of Science in Copenhagen, and the publication is Collins and Evans (2017a).

20. Becker (1953).

21. See Romney, Weller, and Batchelder (1986) for a quantitative argument focused on similar problems. I think, nevertheless, that Romney et al.'s argument does not get to the philosophical heart of the matter. Furthermore, this uniformity is understood tacitly, not explicitly, which means it cannot be investigated through the kind of questioning they use.

22. See Tovey and Adams (2001).

23. For an example of how Imitation Game research explores the extent to which medical professionals are able to develop interactional expertise in the illness experience of patients, see Evans and Crocker (2013).

24. See "The Irish Redhead Convention Takes Place in County Cork," BBC News, August 25, 2014, http://www.bbc.co.uk/news/magazine-28794036.

25. The notion of saturation in qualitative studies (Strauss & Corbin, 1998) also applies here.

Chapter 10

1. Berger (1963). See also Collins, Evans, and Weinel (2017) and Collins et al. (manuscript under submission).

2. I have always thought that actor-network theory falls into the same trap as the philosophical antirelativists—using what are scientific findings as though they could contribute unproblematically to sociological analysis; see Collins and Yearley (1992). The very popular, in STS, "new materialism" also seems to be a prime example of this tendency.

3. For what I believe to be just one example of this kind of thing, where I believe both the nature of expertise in general and the nature of the research on expertise that was claimed to be showing us the truth of the matter were misdescribed, see the exchange represented by Coopmans and Button (2014) and Collins and Evans (2014a).

4. For example, a paper attempting to demarcate fringe science from mainstream science according to institutional grounds was rejected by one of the main journals in social studies of science on the grounds that it was incompatible with the basic rationale of the subject. See Collins, Bartlett, and Reyes-Galindo (2017).

5. See Merton (1942).

6. See Collins and Evans (2002, 2017b), and Collins et al. (manuscript under submission).

7. Though the debate about the nature of science happens at a lower level of the fractal as far as the social scientists are concerned.

8. Collins (2014); Collins and Evans (2017b); Collins et al. (manuscript under submission).

9. This was written up in Collins (1982), a paper called "Special Relativism: The Natural Attitude," and more recently is a view that is central to Collins and Evans (2017b), *Why Democracies Need Science*.

10. Collins, Evans, and Weinel (2017).

11. The original paper setting out the idea of the Third Wave is Collins and Evans (2002).

Chapter 11

1. Brubaker (2002). I know from personal communication with Rogers Brubaker that the more extreme interpretations of his work that I have encountered are not what he intends; his warnings should be restricted to the particular cases of ethnic conflict he deals with.

2. The quotation is taken from Brubaker (2002), p. 164.

3. Books such as Collins (2013, 2017).

4. See Polanyi (1958).

5. Collins and Evans (2002).

6. Another item that could have been added to this lifetime list of projects is a coauthored book on refereeing and umpiring (Collins, Evans, & Higgins, 2016), but that is a one-off and doesn't quite fit the "one developing science" scheme.

References

Abbott, B. P., et al. (2017). GW170817: Observation of gravitational waves from a binary neutron star inspiral. *Physical Review Letters, 119*, 161101.

Anderson, L. (2006). Analytic autoethnography. *Journal of Contemporary Ethnography, 35*(4), 373–395.

Ashmore, M. (1989). *The reflexive thesis: Wrighting sociology of scientific knowledge.* Chicago: University of Chicago Press.

Barrow, J. D. (1999). *Impossibility: The limits of science and the science of limits.* New York: Oxford University Press.

Becker, H. S. (1953). Becoming a marihuana user. *American Journal of Sociology, 59*, 235–242.

Benjamin, D. J., Berger, J. O., Johannesson, M., Nosek, B. A., Wagenmakers, E.-J., Berk, R., et al. (2018). Redefine statistical significance. *Nature Human Behaviour, 2*, 6–10. doi:10.1038/s41562-017-0189-z.

Berger, P. (1963). *Invitation to sociology: A humanistic perspective.* Harmondsworth: Penguin.

Biernacki, R. (2012). *Reinventing evidence in social inquiry: Decoding facts and variables.* New York: Palgrave Macmillan.

Bloor, D. (1973). Wittgenstein and Mannheim on the sociology of mathematics. *Studies in History and Philosophy of Science, 4*, 173–191.

Boden, M. A. (2008). *Mind as machine: A history of cognitive science.* Oxford: Clarendon Press.

Brubaker, R. (2002). Ethnicity without groups. *Archives Européennes de Sociologie, 43*(2), 163–189.

Clarke, B., Gillies, D., Illari, P., Russo, F., & Williamson, J. (2014). Mechanism and the evidence hierarchy. *Topoi, 33*, 339–360.

Collins, H. (1975). The seven sexes: A study in the sociology of a phenomenon, or The replication of experiments in physics. *Sociology, 9*(2), 205–224.

Collins, H. (1981a). What is TRASP? The Radical Programme as a methodological imperative. *Philosophy of the Social Sciences, 11*, 215–224.

Collins, H. (1981b). Son of seven sexes: The social destruction of a physical phenomenon. *Social Studies of Science, 11*, 33–62.

Collins, H. (1981c). Stages in the Empirical Programme of relativism: Introduction to *Social Studies of Science, 11*(1), Special Issue: "Knowledge and Controversy: Studies in Modern Natural Science," 3–10.

Collins, H. (1982). Special relativism: The natural attitude. *Social Studies of Science, 12*, 139–143.

Collins, H. (1985). *Changing order: Replication and induction in scientific practice.* London: Sage.

Collins, H. (1988). Public experiments and displays of virtuosity: The core-set revisited. *Social Studies of Science, 18*, 725–748.

Collins, H. (1990). *Artificial experts: Social knowledge and intelligent machines.* Cambridge, MA: MIT Press.

Collins, H. (1992). *Changing order: Replication and induction in scientific practice.* 2nd ed. Chicago: University of Chicago Press.

Collins, H. (1998). Socialness and the undersocialized conception of society. *Science, Technology, & Human Values, 23*(4), Special Issue: "Humans, Animals, and Machines," 494–516.

Collins, H. (2004a). *Gravity's shadow: The search for gravitational waves.* Chicago: University of Chicago Press.

Collins, H. (2004b). How do you know you've alternated? *Social Studies of Science, 34*(1), 103–106.

Collins, H. (2007). Mathematical understanding and the physical sciences. In H. Collins (Ed.), *Studies in History and Philosophy of Science, 38*(4), Special Issue: "Case Studies of Expertise and Experience," 667–685.

Collins, H. (2008). Actors' and analysts' categories in the social analysis of science. In P. Meusburger, M. Welker, & E. Wunder (Eds.), *Clashes of knowledge* (pp. 1–110). Dordrecht: Springer.

Collins, H. (2010). *Tacit and explicit knowledge.* Chicago: University of Chicago Press.

Collins, H. (2011a). *Gravity's ghost: Scientific discovery in the twenty-first century.* Chicago: University of Chicago Press.

Collins, H. (2011b). Language and practice. *Social Studies of Science, 41*(2), 271–300. doi:10.1177/0306312711399665.

Collins, H. (2013). *Gravity's ghost and big dog: Scientific discovery and social analysis in the twenty-first century.* Chicago: University of Chicago Press.

Collins, H. (2014). *Are we all scientific experts now?* Cambridge: Polity Press.

Collins, H. (2016a). The notion of incommensurability. In A. Blum, K. Gavroglu, & J. Renn (Eds.), *Towards a history of the history of science: 50 years since "Structure"* (pp. 253–258). Berlin: Max Planck Research Library for the History and Development of Knowledge.

Collins, H. (2016b). Reproducibility of experiments: The experimenter's regress, the statistical uncertainty principle and the replication imperative. In H. Atmanspacher & S. Maasen (Eds.), *Reproducibility: Principles, problems and practices* (pp. 65–81). Hoboken, NJ: Wiley.

Collins, H. (2017). *Gravity's kiss: The detection of gravitational waves.* Cambridge, MA: MIT Press.

Collins, H. (2018). *Artifictional intelligence: Against humanities surrender to computers.* Cambridge: Polity Press.

Collins, H. (Forthcoming). The concept of alternation and the sociology of scientific knowledge. In M. Pfadenhauer & H. Knoblauch, *Social constructivism as paradigm: The legacy of the social construction of reality.* Henley-on-Thames: Routledge.

Collins, H. (Manuscript under submission). The detection of gravitational waves: A reflection.

Collins, H., Bartlett, A., & Reyes-Galindo, L. (2017). Demarcating fringe science for policy. *Perspectives on Science 25*(4), 411–438. (An earlier version promulgated as "The Ecology of Fringe Science and Its Bearing on Policy" can be found at https://arxiv.org/abs/1606.05786.)

Collins, H., & Evans, R. (2002). The Third Wave of science studies: Studies of expertise and experience. *Social Studies of Science, 32*(2), 235–296.

Collins, H., & Evans, R. (2007). *Rethinking expertise.* Chicago: University of Chicago Press.

Collins, H., & Evans, R. (2014a). Actor and analyst: A response to Coopmans and Button. *Social Studies of Science, 44*(5), 786–792.

Collins, H., & Evans, R. (2014b). Quantifying the tacit: The Imitation Game and social fluency. *Sociology, 48*(1), 3–19. doi:10.1177/0038038512455735.

Collins, H., & Evans, R. (2015a). Expertise revisited I—Interactional expertise. *Studies in History and Philosophy of Science, 54*, 113–123. (A preprint is available at https://arxiv.org/abs/1611.04423.)

Collins, H., & Evans, R. (2016). A thousand words is worth a picture. *Social Studies of Science, 46*(2), 312–324.

Collins, H., & Evans, R. (2017a). Probes, surveys and the ontology of the social. *Journal of Mixed Methods Research, 11*(3), 328–341. doi:10.1177/1558689815619825.

Collins, H., & Evans, R. (2017b). *Why democracies need science.* Cambridge: Polity Press.

Collins, H., Evans, R., Durant, D., and Weinel, M. (Manuscript under submission). Populism, science and democracy.

Collins, H., Evans, R., & Gorman, M. (2007). Trading zones and interactional expertise. In H. Collins (Ed.), *Studies in History and Philosophy of Science, 38*(4), Special Issue: "Case Studies of Expertise and Experience," 657–666.

Collins, H., Evans, R., & Gorman, M. (2017). Trading zones revisited. arXiv:1712.06327.

Collins, H., Evans, R., & Higgins, C. (2016). *Bad call: Technology's attack on referees and umpires and how to fix it.* Cambridge, MA: MIT Press.

Collins, H., Evans, R., Ribeiro, R., & Hall, M. (2006). Experiments with interactional expertise. *Studies in History and Philosophy of Science, 37*(4), 656–674.

Collins, H., Evans, R., & Weinel, M. (2017). STS as science or politics? *Social Studies of Science, 47*(4), 580–586.

Collins, H., Evans, R., Weinel, M., Lyttleton-Smith, J., Bartlett, A., & Hall, M. (2017). The Imitation Game and the nature of mixed methods. *Journal of Mixed Methods Research, 11*(4), 510–527.

Collins, H., Green, R. H., & Draper, R. C. (1985). Where's the expertise: Expert systems as a medium of knowledge transfer. In M. J. Merry (Ed.), *Expert Systems 85* (pp. 323–334). Cambridge: Cambridge University Press.

Collins, H., Hall, M., Evans, R., Weinel, M., & O'Mahoney, H. (Manuscript in preparation). *Imitation Games: A new method of investigating societies.* Cambridge, MA: MIT Press.

Collins, H., & Harrison, R. (1975). Building a TEA laser: The caprices of communication. *Social Studies of Science, 5,* 441–450.

Collins, H., & Kusch, M. (1998). *The shape of actions: What humans and machines can do.* Cambridge, MA: MIT Press.

Collins, H., Leonard-Clarke, W., & O'Mahoney, H. (2016). Uhm, er: How meaning varies between speech and its typed transcript. arXiv:1609.01207.

Collins, H., & Pinch, T. J. (1981). Rationality and paradigm allegiance in extraordinary science. In H. P. Duerr (Ed.), *The scientist and the irrational* (pp. 284–306). Frankfurt: Syndikat.

Collins, H., & Pinch, T. J. (1982). *Frames of meaning: The social construction of extraordinary science*. Henley-on-Thames: Routledge and Kegan Paul.

Collins, H., & Pinch, T. J. (1993). *The golem: What everyone should know about science*. Cambridge: Cambridge University Press. (New edition, 1998.)

Collins, H., & Pinch, T. (2005). *Dr Golem: How to think about medicine*. Chicago: University of Chicago Press.

Collins, H., & Sanders, G. (2007). They give you the keys and say "drive it": Managers, referred expertise, and other expertises. In H. Collins (Ed.), *Studies in History and Philosophy of Science*, *38*(4), Special Issue: "Case Studies of Expertise and Experience," 621–641.

Collins, H., & Weinel, M. (2011). Transmuted expertise: How technical non-experts can assess experts and expertise. *Argumentation*, *25*(3), Special Issue: "Rethinking Arguments from Experts," 401–413. doi:10.1007/s10503-011-9217-8.

Collins, H., & Yearley, S. (1992). Epistemological chicken. In A. Pickering (Ed.), *Science as practice and culture* (pp. 301–326). Chicago: University of Chicago Press.

Coopmans, C., & Button, G. (2014). Eyeballing expertise. *Social Studies of Science*, *44*(5), 758–785.

Cotgrove, S. (1968). *The science of society*. London: Allen & Unwin.

Dean, L. G., Kendal, R. L., Schapiro, S. J., Thierry, B., & Laland, K. N. (2012). Identification of the social and cognitive processes underlying human cumulative culture. *Science*, *335*, 1114–1118.

Duhem, P. (1981). *The aim and structure of physical theory* (P. P. Wiener, Trans.). New York: Athenaeum.

Durkheim, E. (1915). *Elementary forms of the religious life*. London: Allen & Unwin.

Evans, R., & Crocker, H. (2013). The Imitation Game as a method for exploring knowledge(s) of chronic illness. *Methodological Innovations Online*, *8*(1), 34–52.

Festinger, L., Riecken, H. W., & Schachter, S. (1956). *When prophecy fails*. New York: Harper.

Fine, G. A. (1979). Small groups and culture creation: The idioculture of little league baseball teams. *American Sociological Review*, *44*(5), 733–745.

Fine, G. A. (2007). *Authors of the storm: Meteorologists and the culture of prediction*. Chicago: University of Chicago Press.

Franklin, A. (2013). *Shifting standards: Experiments in particle physics in the twentieth century*. Pittsburgh: University of Pittsburgh Press.

Galison, P. (1997). *Image and logic: A material culture of microphysics*. Chicago: University of Chicago Press.

Garfinkel, H. (1967). *Studies in ethnomethodology*. Upper Saddle River, NJ: Prentice-Hall.

Geertz, C. (1973). *The interpretation of cultures*. New York: Basic Books.

Giles, J. (2006). Sociologist fools physics judges. *Nature 442*:8.

Hartland, J. (1996). Automating blood pressure measurements: The division of labour and the transformation of method. *Social Studies of Science, 26*, 71–94.

Ioannidis, J. P. A. (2005). Why most published research findings are false. *PLOS Medicine, 2*(8), 696–701. doi:10.1371/journal.pmed.0020124.

Kaiser, D. (2011). *How the hippies saved physics: Science, counterculture, and the quantum revival*. New York: W. W. Norton.

Kluckhohn, R. (Ed.). (1962). *Culture and behavior: Collected essays of Clyde Kluckhohn*. Glencoe, IL: Free Press of Glencoe.

Kuhn, T. S. (1962). *The structure of scientific revolutions*. Chicago: University of Chicago Press.

Labinger, J., & Collins, H. (Eds.). (2001). *The one culture? A conversation about science*. Chicago: University of Chicago Press.

Lakatos, I., & Musgrave, A. (Eds.). (1970). *Criticism and the growth of knowledge*. Cambridge: Cambridge University Press.

Latour, B., & Woolgar, S. (1979). *Laboratory life: The social construction of scientific facts*. London: Sage.

Lyons, L. (2013). Discovering the significance of 5 sigma. arXiv:1310.1284 [physics.data-an].

McHugh, P. (1971). On the failure of positivism. In J. D. Douglas (Ed.), *Understanding everyday life* (pp. 337–354). London: Routledge and Kegan Paul.

Medawar, P. B. (1990). Is the scientific paper a fraud? In D. Pyke (Ed.), *The threat and the glory: Reflections on science and scientists* (pp. 228–233). Oxford: Oxford University Press.

Merton, R. K. (1942). Science and technology in a democratic order. *Journal of Legal and Political Sociology, 1*, 115–126.

Mulkay, M., Potter, J., & Yearley, S. (1983). Why an analysis of scientific discourse is needed. In K. D. Knorr-Cetina & M. Mulkay, *Science observed: Perspectives on the social study of science* (pp. 171–203). London: Sage.

Pinch, T. (1981). The sun-set: The presentation of certainty in scientific life. *Social Studies of Science, 1*(11), 131–158.

Pinch, T. (1986). *Confronting nature: The sociology of solar-neutrino detection*. Dordrecht: Reidel.

Polanyi, M. (1958). *Personal knowledge*. London: Routledge and Kegan Paul.

Porter, T. M. (1996). Trust in numbers. Princeton, NJ: Princeton University Press.

Rodrigo, R., & Francisco, L. (2016). The value of practice: A critique of interactional expertise. *Social Studies of Science, 46*(2), 282–311.

Romney, A. K., Weller, S. C., & Batchelder, W. H. (1986). Culture as consensus: A theory of culture and informant accuracy. *American Anthropologist, 88*, 313–338.

Sacks, O. (1985). *The man who mistook his wife for a hat*. London: Duckworth.

Schutz, A. (1964). *Collected papers II: Studies in social theory*. The Hague: Martinus Nijhoff.

Sibum, H. O. (1995). Reworking the mechanical value of heat: Instruments of precision and gestures of accuracy in early Victorian England. *Studies in History and Philosophy of Science, 26*(1), 73–106.

Smith, G. C. S., & Pell, J. P. (2003). Parachute use to prevent death and major trauma related to gravitational challenge: Systematic review of randomised control trials. *British Medical Journal, 327*, 1459–1461.

Stolzenberg, G. (2004). Kinder, gentler science wars. *Social Studies of Science, 34*(1), 77–89.

Strauss, A. L., & Corbin, J. M. (1998). *Basics of qualitative research: Techniques and procedures for developing grounded theory* (2nd ed.). Thousand Oaks, CA: Sage.

Tovey, P., & Adams, J. (2001). Primary care as intersecting social worlds. *Social Science & Medicine, 52*, 695–706.

Turing, A. M. (1950). Computing machinery and intelligence. *Mind, 59*(236), 433–460.

Webb, E. J., Campbell, D. T., Schwartz, R. D., & Sechrest, L. (2000). *Unobtrusive measures* (rev. ed.). Thousand Oaks: Sage Publications.

Wilson, B. (Ed.). (1970). *Rationality*. Oxford: Blackwell.

Winch, P. G. (1958). *The idea of a social science*. London: Routledge and Kegan Paul.

Wittgenstein, L. (1953). *Philosophical investigations*. Oxford: Blackwell.

Wrong, D. H. (1961). The oversocialized conception of man in modern sociology. *American Sociological Review, 26*(2), 183–193.

Yinger, J. M. (1982). *Countercultures: The promise and the peril of a world turned upside down*. New York: Free Press.

Index